To all of my past and current clients,

Thank you for giving me the opportunity to serve you and your financial needs. I can only hope you have enjoyed the journey as much as I have. Unlike managing institutional money, managing money for individuals and families gives me great satisfaction and confidence in knowing that proper wealth management decisions do make a difference.

CONTENTS

INTRODUCTION

Millionaires aren't as rare as they used to be. It's becoming more common for people to amass a net worth of $1 million or more by the time they retire. In addition—considering factors such as lifestyle, cost of living, and life expectancy—many of us will want to save that much or possibly more in order to retire in comfort.

"Middle class" is a bit of a vague term these days. It conveys a level of wealth somewhere shy of upper class but above poverty, which is a pretty vast range. The term "middle class" could also describe your everyday dedicated, hard-working people. It can mean different things to different people.

Put the two terms together—*middle-class millionaire*—and you have a description that has a more specific, though still somewhat flexible, meaning. I use it to refer to people who have accumulated $1 million or more in investable assets, but who don't live a lavish lifestyle. The two are not incongruous. In fact, it's the lifelong habit of living within one's means, working hard, and saving diligently that has paved the way for many middle-class millionaires to enjoy lifelong financial security.

This book, *Middle-Class Millionaire: Surprisingly Simple Strategies to Grow and Enjoy Your Wealth*, is my attempt to take what I've learned in 30 years of working with middle-class millionaires and share those lessons with the broader public, with fellow middle-class millionaires, and with those who aspire to become one eventually.

Writing this book has required me to self-reflect, observe case studies I've worked on, and led me to make various conclusions. In the following pages, I blend general financial and investment education with real-life examples, though the names of clients and other individuals have been changed for obvious privacy reasons.

I hope that you enjoy reading about and learning a few lessons from middle-class millionaires who could be your neighbor, your doctor, your child's school teacher, a business owner, or perhaps a friend or relative.

The key commonality shared by all of the different, successful people described in this book is their ability to work hard, live within their means, manage their money responsibly, and save steadily. Their reward is that today—in their 50s, 60s, and beyond—they can retire or begin to scale back their work responsibilities (or dream about doing so) and enjoy the next phase of their journey. In this next period of their lives, they'll transition from working to enjoying their leisure time. They will no longer actively accumulate wealth, but instead work to sustain their wealth while enjoying their retirement. Additionally, they may plan how best to pass on some of their good fortune to their heirs when their journey is over.

Are you a middle-class millionaire? Would you like to become one? You can learn how in this book.

CLARK A. KENDALL
CFA, AEP®, CFP®
FOUNDER AND CEO OF KENDALL CAPITAL
ROCKVILLE, MARYLAND

SECTION I

How to Accumulate Wealth

CHAPTER 1
The Mindset of a Saver

Some people who earn relatively modest salaries manage to accumulate millions of dollars in savings throughout their lives while others—even those who earn sizeable salaries—never seem to save. Perhaps you've heard stories about star athletes or other celebrities who earned millions, but burned through it all, eventually ending up barely able to make ends meet.

Household names who've gone from wealth to bankruptcy or foreclosure include Michael Jackson, Mike Tyson, M.C. Hammer, Kim Basinger, and even Mark Twain.[1]

How can these people come into so much money, but see it slip through their fingers? What is different about savers? How do they do it? What can we all learn from them?

Looking at the formula, it's not rocket science. Spend less than you earn. Save early and regularly. So, why is it so easy for some people and seemingly impossible for others?

Let's look at the paths of a saver versus a spender.

JOHN, THE ENGINEER: HIS MONEY GREW AND GREW

For the past 20 years, I managed money for John, an engineer who retired from a large telecommunications firm in the mid-1980s with a modest pension of around $30,000 per year and annual Social Security benefits of $24,000. John's wife, Sue, died in the late 1990s. We took over the family investment portfolio of $600,000 in 2000. Here's how John and his wife saved their money: Up until retirement, they saved 10 percent of his salary, gave to charities, and lived modestly off the rest of their income for most of their working lives.

Note the order of priorities listed here: save, give, and then modestly spend what's left. What's also important is that they started this process early in their lives together, which allowed their savings plenty of time to grow.

When John died in 2017 at age 96, he left behind a $2 million investment portfolio. Before passing, John remarked to me several times that he didn't understand how he could receive more than $100,000 of dividend income per year when he had never earned more than $40,000 per year during his career. Those relatively small amounts saved early in their lives and a lifetime of living modestly allowed them to accumulate wealth and made a huge difference during his retirement.

DEBBIE AND STEVE: PAYING FOR
THEIR SLOW START AS SAVERS

I recall a commercial for oil filters in which the message is to maintain your vehicle cost-efficiently by changing your car's oil regularly along with the oil filter. What's the consequence of not doing that?

Well, the tagline said it all: "You can pay me now," said the guy who could change your oil for a few dollars. "Or, you can pay *me* later," said the expensive mechanic who rebuilds car engines that had been neglected.

The same applies to saving for retirement and for life's other major expenses. John—the retired engineer who saved steadily—reaped the rewards for his disciplined savings plan, and then passed on the benefits to his children and grandchildren. In sharp contrast to John's example, we have worked with several couples who waited longer than they should have to start to save for retirement. How long? Well, Debbie and Steve waited until they were in their 50s to start saving earnestly for their so-called "golden years."

They were always busy paying for other things: the mortgage on their 4,500-square feet, five-bedroom house with the four full bathrooms and three-car garage in the desirable neighborhood; the private school tuition for their four children; the annual vacations to the Caribbean or Mediterranean…it wasn't necessarily a lavish lifestyle, compared to some people, but their attitude was to live now. "Why deny yourself the pleasures of life when you can afford them?" That was their prevailing philosophy about money.

Well, they learned "why" a little late. As retirement age grew closer, they started to realize that they should be saving seriously for their future. I met with them in their early 50s and helped them to begin saving in earnest—otherwise, they'd never retire. So, they started making retirement savings their number one priority rather than what they'd been doing before—adding a bit of money now and then when they had some extra money available.

At least they had realized by then that they couldn't do *everything* with their money. They asked their children to contribute to their college education. They went on fewer and more modest vacations. They downsized once their kids were out of their home, and they managed to buy a smaller home with a modest mortgage given the equity they'd built. So, in that regard, their investment paid off.

Despite eventually making better choices to improve their financial well-being, they truly needed to save hard to play catch up. At that time, Steve earned roughly $110,000 as a lawyer and Debbie earned $70,000 as a nurse. By saving 20 percent of their $180,000 in combined salaries—roughly $36,000 per year—with matching 401(k) employer contributions of about $5,400 annually, and with the benefit of generally positive investment market returns since they buckled down to save in 2002, they're now on track to boost what was a very modest $70,000 retirement nest egg at age 50 to an estimated $1.5 million by the time they turn 70.

Yes, by the time they turn 70.

How much are they projected to have by age 65, which is just three years from now? Close to $1 million in total savings. That might not sound too bad, but if you follow the rule of thumb that you can safely withdraw 4 percent of your retirement nest egg principle at retirement in order for it to have a very strong chance of lasting 30 years, that would only provide them with $40,000 in annual retirement account withdrawals. Add to that the estimated Social Security benefits of roughly $57,000 a year,[2] and the combined $97,000 would fall far shy of what they'd need to maintain their lifestyle, roughly $144,000, or 80 percent of their current gross earnings of $180,000 a year.

By working another five years, Debbie and Steve can keep adding $36,000 a year plus matching contributions, all of which will compound on top of the $1 million. Also, by delaying taking Social Security benefits from age 66 to 70, Debbie and Steve will increase their projected annual combined benefits by 32 percent, from $57,000 to about $75,000.

Et voilà! That's not just the name of the nice Belgian-French restaurant where Debbie and Steve like to dine in Washington, D.C. With those five extra years of work and delaying withdrawing benefits, they'll be able to retire in the lifestyle they're used to. They'll be able to withdraw $61,000 a year from their retirement accounts for a total annual retirement income of roughly $136,000—not quite their $144,000 target, but close. They will also have four fewer years in retirement to fund, which means less risk of outliving their money.

It helps greatly that Debbie and Steve are confident that they will still be able to work into their late 60s or beyond. Also, they each enjoy their jobs for the most part, but not everyone is that fortunate. Many pre-retirees plan on working longer, but failing health or economic realities—such as a company downsizing—can get in the way of those best-laid plans.

Compare the choices and sacrifices made by John and Sue, the early diligent savers, with those of Debbie and Steve, the couple who lived large and then, despite earning good salaries, had to save aggressively and who will have to work an extra few years.

I hope you agree that it's far better, safer, and easier to adopt the mindset of a saver early on. To paraphrase that oil filter ad, "You can save now, or save more later."

Let's look at that saver's mindset and take away a few lessons:

1. Save first. Then spend. If you "pay yourself first" and put away a certain percentage of your paycheck every pay period, you'll never see that money and you'll never be tempted to spend it. You can do this through automatic payroll deductions at work via your human resources department or payroll administrator, or you can arrange to have your bank automatically transfer money into your retirement account each month or however frequently makes sense for you. If your employer does not offer a retirement plan, you can utilize a variety of Individual Retirement Accounts (IRAs). Everyone can do this, and it's simple and painless.

2. Live below your means. This is an attitude more than anything. Adopt the attitude of not needing to keep up with the Joneses, and not needing a new luxury car every three years, or not needing to buy the biggest house you can afford. In other words, create a lifestyle in which you can save and enjoy yourself. If you earn a decent middle-class or upper middle-class salary of $80,000 or $120,000 or $160,000 per year, but spend *less than you earn*, your money will grow and you'll accumulate wealth. It's simple math. Well, actually, it's compounding math!

3. Start early. Compound interest or compound returns is one of the most powerful forces in the world. Let's assume you began saving 10 percent of your $40,000 salary at age 22, or $4,000 per year, and continued saving that percentage in a 401(k). Then, let's say you receive an employer matching contribution of 50 percent of the first 6 percent of your salary that you contribute, and your employer continues to match your contributions as your salary increases annually by 3 percent. That bonus can make an enormous difference over time. If your money earned a modest 7 percent per year on average, by the time you turn 65, you'd have $1,993,477 in savings according to the 401(k) calculator at dinkytown.net.[3]

That's it. It's not rocket science. To recap, remember three things:

- Save first.

- Live below your means.

- Start early.

By adopting these simple habits, dictated by a saver's mindset, almost anyone can create and maintain a healthy financial life before and after retirement. It's not how much you earn—it's how much you save that will lead you to a financially healthy retirement.

CHAPTER 2
Formula for Success

What does financial success mean for you? Perhaps living without financial worries? Having enough to live on for the rest of your life without having to sacrifice any basics? Or perhaps it means accumulating enough wealth that you can pass on a substantial amount to your heirs?

However you define success, some basic formulas and rules of thumb can help point the way and help you reach your goals.

APPLY THE POWER OF TIME AND MONEY

You've probably heard the expression "time is money." It typically refers to the value of one's time that could be spent making money, which makes time itself valuable.

Given the tendency for investments—even somewhat risky ones—to rise in value over time, there's a basic tenet of lifelong investing for a goal such as retirement: the sooner you begin to save, the sooner your money can begin earning more money through compounding returns. The more money you save sooner, the more you'll have later.

To help illustrate this, there's a simple and effective rule of thumb: the Rule of 72. It can be a great planning tool and wonderful source of inspiration.

FOLLOW THE RULE OF 72

The Rule of 72 is a simplified way to determine how long an investment will take to double at any particular fixed annual rate of interest. You just divide 72 by your investment's annual rate of return to get a rough estimate of how many years it would take for your initial investment to double in size; then, how many years it would take to double again and again, and so on. The earlier you begin, and the more your investment earns annually, the more you'll have by the time you need the money.

Let's see how this works. Assume you invest $10,000 at a 9 percent annual return. Divide 72 by the number nine, and it will double in just eight years.

So, if you invest $10,000 at age 22, at a 9 percent rate of return, it'll grow to:

$20,000 by age 30
$40,000 by age 38
$80,000 by age 46
$160,000 by age 54
$320,000 by age 62
$640,000 by age 70

Note how much this savings grows in the final two eight-year doubling periods. It quadruples, and grows by an impressive

$480,000 from age 54 to 70. Let's assume you would like to have $500,000 as a retirement nest egg. You'd be far from your goal at age 54, and you'd still be shy of it at age 62, with just $320,000. By continuing to work and invest—and therefore not needing to draw down your savings—until you reach 70, you'd be fine.

Now, let's play with the rule, which you can do easily enough with an interactive online calculator. What if you only started saving at age 38, using the same assumed 9 percent rate of return? Your $10,000 would double by age 46, double again by 54, and double twice more by age 70, but you'd only have $160,000 saved. So, by starting to save as soon as you can, you open the possibility of having enormous rewards later in life thanks to compound growth.

Of course, this illustration is not typical of real life. A realistic savings scenario would involve adding to your savings account each year, making it much easier to reach a goal of $1 million or $2 million or more. However, the principle remains that for lifelong retirement savings, let time be on your side.

LOOK AT HOW SLOWLY CONSERVATIVE
INVESTMENTS GROW

We can also use the Rule of 72 to show the benefit of investing fairly aggressively—or more suitably—for long-term goals. By that, I mean having a higher allocation to stocks, and less to bonds and cash or cash-equivalent investments, such as money market funds.

For example, at a 3 percent annual return, it would take 24 years for your money to double (72÷3=24). So, assuming the same $10,000 invested at age 22, it would double to $20,000 at 46 and only $40,000 at age 70. Compare that to the $640,000 in the example based on a 9 percent annual return. It's obvious which savings plan you'd rather take!

RISK AND RETURN: MANAGE THEM WELL

This invites a discussion about risk because investments that offer a higher potential return, such as stocks, come with more volatility. The reason risk and return tend to go hand in hand is that investors are generally compensated for investing in higher-risk investments such as stocks, real estate, commodities, or other non-guaranteed investments that can fluctuate in value. Conversely, if you're taking low levels of risk in a certificate of deposit or short-term government bond, you can't expect to earn much of a return.

Understandably, some of us are more risk tolerant while others are naturally more risk averse. It's important to recognize your personal comfort level with risk, and there are plenty of helpful risk-tolerance quizzes and exercises that you can do.

Even given that variance in risk tolerance, generally speaking, short-term goals—let's say a purchase you're saving for in the next year or two—call for an investment with less volatility. This safer investment will tend to have much more modest returns.

On the other hand, for longer-term goals (such as retirement or even college savings for a young child), when you have 10 or more years for your investment to ride the market's ups and downs, you can afford to invest more aggressively without taking on much more risk because you will have more time to recover from any market downturns.

For example, let's look at the stock market at the beginning of the most recent financial crisis. We can use the S&P 500 Index as a market proxy. It stood at 1565 on October 9, 2007,[1] before the sub-prime mortgage crisis and associated market turbulence led to the full-fledged crisis in late 2008 that led to the market's low point on March 9, 2009, when the S&P 500 closed at a low of 676. That's a drop of 57 percent in 17 months.[2]

If you were near retirement and heavily invested in stocks, you might have seen your savings cut in half, with no time to recover. Yet, if you were 10 or more years away from needing that money and could leave it invested in the market, by year-end of 2017—roughly a decade after the market downturn began—you'd have made up all of your losses and tacked on 70 percent more in gains after a very turbulent decade. By that point, the S&P 500 had climbed to 2,673.61.[3] So, assuming you had $1 million in stock investments 10 years earlier, rather than see half of it disappear, you might be looking at roughly $1.7 million just because you stayed focused on your long-term goal and weathered the storm.

Consider the nervousness that many investors felt at the depths of the market downturn in the winter of 2009, just before stocks began to recover. From its ebb on March 9, 2009, the S&P 500 gained almost 400 percent in the following eight years and nine months.

What truly matters is *time in the market* rather than *market timing.* That's because no one can really know what will happen to investments in the next month or even the next year. Over the next 10, 20, or 30 years, generally we can expect investments to rise, and more aggressive investments will most likely earn more. Of course, there are no guarantees, but that's what has occurred over longer periods again and again.

DOLLAR-COST AVERAGING CAN HELP KEEP YOU ON TRACK

One way to help stay on track toward a long-term goal, such as retirement, is through a methodical regular approach to saving. By contributing steadily to your retirement account through dollar-cost averaging—that means investing the same dollar value at regular intervals, such as $400 every month—your savings habit is instilled.

This also helps you to take advantage of market downturns and in effect buy investments at a discount. For example, $400 would buy twice as many shares of a stock at $20 per share than it would at $40 per share. No guarantees, again, but by systematically investing, you are more likely to purchase stocks at low points when you otherwise might not have the stomach to invest. In fact, this could help you flip your reaction to a market downturn and put your mind at ease if you don't need the money in the near term. Rather than be worried and second-guess your investments, you can learn to see downturns as an opportunity to buy more of a given investment than you would at a market peak.

WHAT RISKS ARE RELEVANT TO YOU?

Let's revisit the notion of risk or the variety of risks involved with investing. Review the table below and consider which risks matter the most if you're investing for short-term goals versus long-term goals.

SHORT-TERM CONCERNS	LONG-TERM CONCERNS
Day-to-day market volatility	Longevity risk: Outliving your money
Concentrated risk: Investing too much in a single company, industry, sector, or country	Inflation risk: Losing purchasing power over time

For your high school senior student's college fund, or for an auto purchase next year, you'll want something "safe" like a CD or money market fund. But for your retirement 20 or 30 years away, the key risks include inflation and the potential loss of purchasing power, and even more importantly, the risk of outliving your money. Because of those dangers, it can be *less risky* to invest for growth over the long term rather than protecting your principal against market swings.

There are numerous other risks that don't fit neatly into short- or long-term boxes, such as the tendency of many investors to underperform the stock market by buying and selling shares of individual stocks or mutual funds too frequently. First, that can become costly if you're paying commissions or fees, and it may lead to tax inefficiency. Similarly, it can also lead to making poorly considered, emotionally driven decisions. In the next chapter, we'll discuss the many ways that we tend to make mistakes, often based on our emotions.

REMEMBER THESE LESSONS

- Start investing early and give your money more opportunity to grow.

- Invest steadily, taking advantage of dollar-cost averaging to buy at bargain prices when the market dips.

- Expect to take some more investment risks for your longer-term goals. That can be a worthwhile trade-off allowing you to potentially earn higher long-term returns.

- Understand the variety of risks, know what's most relevant to your situation, and manage those risks well.

- Don't overreact to short-term market volatility when your goal is far away.

SECTION II

How to Grow Your Wealth

CHAPTER 3
Financial Literacy

Personal financial literacy is "the ability to use knowledge and skills to manage financial resources effectively for a lifetime of financial well-being," according to the President's Advisory Council on Financial Literacy.[1]

That means being able to understand how to balance a budget, buy a home, fund your children's college education, save for your own retirement, avoid bankruptcy, use debt wisely, and assess and choose from a pool of complex financial products. Furthermore, when the time comes, it means making sure you have enough retirement income for as long as you live.

What are the consequences of not being financially literate? A study by financial services firm TIAA-CREF found that people with high financial literacy do better at planning for retirement and end up with twice as much wealth as those who don't plan for retirement. People with low financial literacy tend to borrow more, pay unnecessary fees for financial products, and pay higher interest fees, leaving them with less wealth in the end.

So, how can we become more financially literate? Start by understanding basic, but important, financial concepts.

See the financial glossary at the back of the book for a list of key terms and definitions. Nevertheless, you need to do more than just know financial terms. You need to be able to make smart financial decisions, which isn't always easy.

LEARN THE LINGO AND APPLY IT WELL

Here are just a few key financial concepts to understand and apply in a way that furthers your financial well-being.

Active versus passive investing

Annuities (variable and fixed)

Asset allocation and asset correlation

Bond coupons, duration, maturity, and credit ratings

Capital gains and losses, and how to offset them to reduce tax liability

Credit ratings and your FICO score, and how to improve them

Life insurance (term and permanent)

Liability insurance and umbrella insurance

Leverage (its advantages and risks)

Stock valuation methodology

Tax-deferred accounts, such as traditional and Roth IRAs, 401(k)s and 403(b)s

For definitions of these and other financial terms, please see the glossary. For more detailed discussions about specific items, read the appropriate chapters further on.

Understanding and being comfortable with these and other important financial terms can help you handle an increasingly complex financial world where individual consumers have to be responsible for their long-term financial well-being more than ever. Corporate pensions are largely a thing of the past, and our expectations of Social Security benefits may need to change.

DON'T BE AFRAID, CONFUSED, OR OVERWHELMED

Don't be intimidated or turned off by jargon or alarmed by sensationalistic headlines and financial reports. They often exist in part to sell publications or boost ratings. Remember that many financial newspapers, magazines, and programs on CNBC exist to earn a profit for their publishers or owners. They need to keep viewership and readership levels high, and that can sometimes mean their interests and yours don't align.

You might hear about a hot stock to buy, or why you should consider getting out of the stock market before it crashes, but you might do better with a thoughtful review of your entire portfolio; or, even better, a discussion with your financial advisor about your long-term goals and whether a gain or drop in the stock market is going to change those goals or call for a change in your investment approach.

BUBBLES BURST

One thing to be aware of is an opportunity bubble and the accompanying notion that "this time is different." We saw it during the dot-com bubble that was hard to resist in the late 1990s. How could you stand on the sidelines and *not* invest in the amazing new, dynamic world of technology and the internet? Well, that bubble burst and a lot of investors wished they had used restraint.

The housing bubble of the mid-2000s, just a half-dozen years later, had such far-reaching consequences that it morphed into a global financial crisis because of opportunistic packaging and reselling of inherently risky sub-prime mortgages. The extent to which collateralized debt obligations were sold throughout global investment markets left huge numbers of unwitting investors vulnerable.

That time *it really was different*. The damage was much more devastating than anyone could have imagined. Many of the people who had the financial acumen to know better—including bond insurers and the salespeople who repackaged and sold tranches of risky assets—didn't use sound judgment. That's because they were caught up in the bubble mentality, looking to make more money rather than focusing on risks to their customers and to their firms.

It's easy to criticize in retrospect, but these bubbles were identifiable. Federal Reserve chairman Alan Greenspan spoke of "irrational exuberance" back in December 1996.[2] That was three years and three months before the NASDAQ Composite Index reached its peak before falling 78 percent in the ensuing 30 months.[3]

Was Bitcoin another bubble? It might not have been clear amid all the fuss in the fall of 2017, but through today's rear-view mirror, look at its sharp rise and fall. Its unit price skyrocketed from $6,447 on Halloween 2017 to $19,343 by December 16th of that same year before crashing. By Halloween 2018, the price was more settled at $6,307 per unit. If you had bought it in October 2017, you might have lost roughly 2 percent, but had you bought it at or near its peak, you might have lost two-thirds of your investment. Now, *that* is scary. Even scarier: By early February 2019, Bitcoin had dropped to below $3,500 per unit, a drop of another 45 percent, or 82 percent below its peak in December 2017!

Looking back now, Bitcoin had all the makings of a bubble:

- The skyrocketing price rise. (Hint: What goes up quickly can sometimes come down just as quickly.)

- The mad dash to invest in something that practically no one understands. ("Irrational exuberance?")

- The risks that come with "the greater fool theory," which is that "the price of an object is determined not by its intrinsic value, but rather by irrational beliefs and expectations of market participants." As long as there's a fool greater than you who is willing to buy what you're selling for an even higher price, then *you* are fine, but is that person going to find a *greater fool*? And if not…?

That's not investing. That's speculation. It's gambling, and it invites very large and painful losses of money. Financial literacy isn't just about understanding the definitions of financial terms.

It's about knowing how vulnerable we are to our emotions and protecting ourselves from our worst impulses. Well, maybe that's financial wisdom, but that wisdom could save you a lot of grief!

Focusing on fundamentals can help. Purchasing stock means buying a share of the ownership of a public company. When deciding what stock and how many shares to purchase, you want to evaluate the expectations of a profit. It's best to try to evaluate profit via formulas such as a stock's price-to-earnings ratio or price-to-sales ratio. It can involve an analysis of a company's revenues, expenses, balance sheet, income statement, and the underlying predictability of its cash flow.

It's also beneficial to understand the basics of behavioral finance and our shortcomings as financial consumers and investors. It's not enough to crunch numbers on balance sheets and income statements. We need to understand what is driving the price of a financial asset higher and whether there is some additional risk associated with that momentum.

UNDERSTAND AND PROTECT AGAINST OUR SHORTCOMINGS

We're human, and that means we are also emotional, and emotions often lead to poorly considered and potentially damaging decisions. Greed and fear both involve an adrenaline rush, and that often doesn't end well. When our investment rises, we can feel elation. We might believe we're smart when really we may just have benefited from dumb luck. When given an opportunity to assess whether to buy or sell a given investment, we tend to sell winners and hold on too long to losers, partly because we don't want to admit that we may have made a mistake.

We can protect ourselves against our own worst emotional impulses by adhering to several rules:

- Avoid making emotionally based financial decisions.

- Consult a trusted advisor. Bounce your ideas off of someone who you respect and trust.

- If you're about to make a big decision, sleep on it! One more day could give you additional clarity and prevent you from making a mistake that you'll regret.

- Have a long-term financial plan and maintain the discipline of that plan.

- View short-term setbacks through the long-term lens appropriate to your goal, and you can turn those setbacks into long-term opportunities.

AVOID OVERCONCENTRATION THROUGH DISCIPLINE

A recurring mistake I often see when we take over the investment management of a "do-it-yourself" middle-class millionaire is improper asset allocation. We inherit many accounts with unbalanced portfolios. They typically have too much money allocated to a single security or sector. It's not unusual for us to inherit a stock portfolio with one security making up more than 50 percent of the entire account value.

Can you just imagine if you had half of your portfolio in General Electric (GE) since the turn of the century? The stock has dropped to one-third of its value while the major indices are three to four times higher. In concrete terms, compare $500,000 in GE dropping in value to $133,000 while an investment in the overall stock market might have grown to $1.5 million or more. In this case, even if the other half of your portfolio grew along with the rest of the market, your overall portfolio would have dramatically underperformed.

When we manage stocks in a portfolio, for the most part, we buy securities in one percent increments until they comprise up to 3 percent of the portfolio. So, on a $1 million portfolio, we would stop buying once a given security reaches $30,000. For securities that perform well, we'll let them rise in value but will proceed to trim them back when they exceed 7 percent of the total portfolio value. This helps prevent the overall portfolio's performance from being overly dependent on any one security.

We also monitor the portfolios to ensure that we don't exceed the respective benchmark's allocation in any one sector by more than 10 percent. This way, if we hold great healthcare stocks and the healthcare sector underperforms over a given period of time, we won't dramatically underperform.

Understand that if your horizon is long-term, market dips or corrections can be buying opportunities for you, in which you are buying investments at a discount. What did legendary investor Warren Buffett do during the financial crisis in 2008? He bought shares of Wall Street investment bank Goldman Sachs at a discount for $5 billion and came away with a $3.1 billion profit in cash and stock for a 62 percent return on a five-year investment,[4] creating more wealth for himself and shareholders of his firm, Berkshire Hathaway, while helping a financial firm in crisis. He's done that type of thing time and again on his way to a net worth of $87 billion by his 88th birthday on August 30, 2018.[5]

Maybe you won't ever become a billionaire like Buffett, but with diligence and discretion, you can become a middle-class millionaire!

REMEMBER THESE LESSONS

- Learn the basic language of finance. Financial literacy correlates with fewer mistakes and greater personal wealth.

- Don't get lured by hype. Maintain a layer of healthy skepticism and refrain from investing in things that you don't understand to help bubble-proof your finances.

- Understand that we are emotional creatures by nature. Try to guard against making emotion-based decisions that can trip you up on your path towards accumulating wealth.

CHAPTER 4

Teach Your Children 12 Life Lessons About Money

Only one in three U.S. states requires high school students to take a course in personal finance, according to a survey by the Council for Economic Education. A 2015 study of nearly 30,000 teenagers from 18 countries found that 22 percent of students in the U.S. failed to reach the baseline level of proficiency in financial literacy, according to the Paris-based Organisation for Economic Co-operation and Development (OECD).[1]

The study also found that on average across the participating OECD countries, 83 percent of students said they discuss money with their parents monthly, weekly, or almost every day. So, whatever you think about the shortcomings of our school system regarding financial education, we all play an important role in teaching our children about money; there are many opportunities to do so from a very young age.

Here are 12 things you can do to teach your children about money. These are lessons with lifelong potential benefits that you can incorporate into your regular routines.

1. Show them savings using a clear jar. As a society, we're using less and less cash. Credit cards, debit cards, PayPal, and auto-payments have largely replaced cash and even check writing for most of our expenses. Make a point of showing your young children cash. What better way than to have a clear jar in which they can save bills and coins? It's better than a piggy bank because they can see their money grow. Consider using three jars: one each for spending, saving, and giving.

2. Give them money. In addition to birthday gifts and money from the tooth fairy, give them an allowance that can be geared for spending, saving, and giving, and make it clear which items you *won't* buy for them but that they can choose to buy themselves. For young kids, this might be checkout-line snacks. This could eliminate grocery store whining if your children know *they* are responsible for buying their own treats, and not you! Teens could use allowance money for clothes or gas for their vehicle. Giving them money with which to budget and plan can be a great teaching tool.

3. Talk about choices. With an allowance comes decision making and, at times, tough choices. Discuss the merits of buying a particular toy or electronics device versus something else with their finite financial resource. Ultimately, let them decide and then live with the consequences.

4. Give them extra earning power. Beyond their basic allowance, which many people feel shouldn't be given for chores, why not give your children opportunities to earn bonus money? Perhaps they could earn it by doing extra chores, such as sweeping out the garage, weeding the garden, or vacuuming and washing your car.

5. *Encourage them to earn money.* When they're old enough—early teens or even preteens—encourage them to earn money on a regular basis doing jobs in the neighborhood like babysitting or dog walking.

6. *Open a bank account.* At a fairly young age, perhaps once they receive a regular allowance, they can have a bank account. You should discuss ways for them to help their account balance grow through saving and interest. The OECD survey found that students who had a bank account had measurably higher financial literacy scores than those of similar socio-economic status who didn't have a bank account. At the same time, however, close to two-thirds of those students with a bank account didn't have the skills to manage the account and couldn't read or understand a bank statement. Granted, these days they're more likely to use an app to check their account balance, which is fine as long as they're tracking their savings, spending, and account balance.

7. *Match their savings.* Let's assume your children have an allowance and a bank account, and they understand the value of saving. Why not encourage them to save the way a 401(k) savings plan sponsor encourages plan participants to save? Match their savings! One way is to give a year-end matching bonus for the amount their bank account balance has grown for the calendar year. If they save $250, you'll match that amount dollar for dollar and raise it to $500.

8. Give them stock. I have four children, and every year since they were young, I've given each of them $500 worth of stock as a financial "stocking stuffer" at Christmas. I gave them shares of Microsoft, Verizon, and PEPCO. When they were young, they moaned and complained, but as they got older and their investments appreciated, their appreciation for these stock gifts grew as well, long after they outgrew their toys.

9. Demonstrate through your example. What could be more effective and powerful than living your message by being financially responsible and staying out of debt? Show them how you evaluate financial decisions. Talk to them about how you manage your money. Talk about the costs of owning a car, including insurance, gas, repairs, and maintenance. Discuss the many costs that come with home ownership: utility expenses, insurance, property taxes, mortgage interest, repairs, and upgrades. Have a two-way conversation, inviting their input about using cash versus debt to pay for consumption items such as cars, vacations, and clothes. Explain why your summer vacation might involve camping or visiting family instead of going to Disney World, taking a cruise, or traveling to Europe.

10. Show them how to budget. Teach them to live within their means. The onus is on you because they're not learning these skills at school. Let them see your budget for household needs and wants, how you make charitable contributions, and how you save for short-term goals as well as college and retirement. These could be the most valuable lessons you teach your children, and it's a defining characteristic of how middle-class millionaire parents teach their children the wisdom of money.

11. Warn them about the dangers of debt. Once your teenagers are about to enter college, they're probably going to be lured with offers for credit cards. While you want to encourage them to build their credit history, work with them to do so wisely and responsibly, incorporating all of the lessons you've helped to teach them up to that point. This is also a good opportunity to be frank and teach them how student loans can be used responsibly, but also lead to problems if they borrow more than can be repaid in a reasonable timeframe.

12. Strongly encourage them to begin retirement saving. As an older teenager, once they're earning enough money in a part-time job to be able to put away even $1,000, get them to open a Roth individual retirement account (IRA). Take them through that Rule of 72 exercise to show how $1,000 invested perhaps in a stock index mutual fund at an early age can grow to $2,000, $4,000, $8,000, $16,000, $32,000, $64,000, et cetera over the years.

CHAPTER 5
Taking Credit

Debt: it's a four-letter word. It can be used to your advantage as well as abused or misused. I've seen clients who were models of good debt management in their personal finances. In fact, many middle-class millionaires have a good handle on this aspect of their finances.

On the other hand, in some cases bad debt management can cost people dearly. For example, when saddled with large student loan repayments, many young professionals find it hard to save in a retirement account or build up a down payment for a home.

YOUR PERSONAL BALANCE SHEET

Picture a personal balance sheet. On the left side are your assets, or things you own. Typically, this includes investments as well as assets such as a home, vehicles, and other property. On the right side are your debts—things you owe. This could include your home mortgage, a car loan, student loans, other personal loans, and credit card debt.

When you borrow money, it's a form of leverage. It allows you to acquire, spend, or invest more than you could by merely using your available cash. For that leverage to help you build wealth rather than depreciate, you should only borrow to invest in assets that appreciate or produce income. Conversely, you should avoid borrowing money—or using this leverage—to pay for consumption items, especially luxury items such as sports cars or vacations.

A LOOK AT GOOD AND BAD DEBT MANAGEMENT

What constitutes good and bad debt?

Good Debt

Is typically used to finance items that are necessities and enhance your well-being. If you want to buy a house or a car, for instance, paying 100 percent cash up front is an unlikely option. This is certainly the case for a house unless you're downsizing and have the proceeds of your existing home to buy the new place.

Involves affordable payments and reasonable interest rates. Compare the interest rate on a home mortgage—typically 4 percent to 5 percent these days—with credit card interest of up to 25 percent. Weigh either of those with what you might expect to earn on bonds (3 percent to 6 percent perhaps) or stocks (8 percent to 10 percent) over the long term. In one case, the rate is reasonable; in the other, it's astronomical.

Payments must be made on time and you shouldn't borrow more than half of your available credit. If you can pay off your credit card balance in full each month, you're taking advantage of a 30-day interest-free loan by the credit card issuer. Even if you have to pay some credit card interest, it helps build your credit score, and you should limit using the card while you're paying off a large balance.

Bad debt

Purchases might not be affordable, don't contribute to your well-being, or are frivolous. Avoid using a credit card or even a personal loan to buy a luxury item that is outside your comfort zone.

Interest rate might be high; monthly payments might be challenging. To be building wealth, you don't want to be bogged down by enormous monthly debts.

Don't borrow just because you can. As a financially astute consumer, you need to assess your debt burden. The bank might approve you for a loan or a mortgage based on their acceptable debt-to-income ratio, but you don't have to take it all. Understand that banks are in the business of making money and they want you to pay them interest as much as possible for as long as possible.

DO YOU WANT TO CARRY A MORTGAGE?

The prevailing wisdom is that borrowing to buy a house is a form of good credit. That's because houses can rise in value, and if you rent and never own, you won't build equity in a home.

There's certainly a trade-off, but consider that the days of rising real estate values from the last half-century might not carry over into the next half-century. You might assume that real estate will gain in value, but that's not something to count on. The price of your home could be stagnant or even fall over lengthy periods of time depending on a lot of market variables.

Therefore, home ownership can make sense for some people, especially if you're looking to put down your roots and stay in a place for many years. Positive intangibles include greater privacy and not having to put up with loud footsteps overhead or boisterous parties just beyond your bedroom wall. Be that as it may, home ownership isn't for everyone. Renting certainly can be easier and free up time that you might spend maintaining or upgrading a home.

On a strictly financial basis, consider that home ownership involves much more than a monthly mortgage. It comes with property taxes, insurance, utility bills, maintenance, and repairs; and all of that can add up. Because of the hefty costs associated with buying and selling a home, it can be much more economical staying in one place for a while rather than moving frequently. We'll discuss how to hunt for a good value even more in the next chapter.

MORTGAGE AS SMART LEVERAGE

Let us compare a couple of 40-year-old former college room-mates, Jack and Tom. More than 15 years after graduating from college, Tom has been paying rent of $2,000 per month in an expensive neighborhood, but has no assets other than a small 401(k) balance. Meanwhile, Jack bought a starter home with a $1,500 monthly mortgage thanks to some help from his parents on the down payment. Even though Jack tied up initial capital in the form of a down payment and has to pay for utilities, real estate taxes, and home maintenance, his living expenses were about the same as Tom's. Though today Jack is now halfway through a 30-year mortgage, and has built about $150,000 of equity that is a now a tangible financial asset that can be used to buy a new house in the expensive neighborhood where Tom lives. He has created this home equity by having the home appreciate in value and by slowing paying down the principal, while also realizing income tax savings by deducting the interest on the mortgage and real estate taxes.

MORTGAGES: MORE ISN'T ALWAYS BETTER

Just because some mortgage debt can help you build equity doesn't mean more mortgage debt is always better. Consider Nick and Jane. They did a major upgrade after moving from a modest home to a large dream home two decades ago. The previous home doubled in price from $250,000 to $500,000 *after* they sold it.

As for the dream home? Today it's worth just about what they paid initially plus the cost of renovations and improvements—$750,000. With more than $10,000 a year in real estate taxes plus assorted other expenses that come with a larger home, they realize today that they might have been better off financially had they stayed in the more modest home and invested some of the additional money in the stock market.

MORTGAGE AS AN EXIT STRATEGY

Owning a home in retirement doesn't always make a lot of sense. First, as you age, you become less and less inclined to mow the lawn, weed the garden, shovel snow, fix the roof, clean the gutters, and on and on. Yet, building equity while working and eventually using that equity to downsize into something smaller and more manageable in retirement can work well. There's also always the possibility of getting a reverse mortgage, in which you convert your equity into income. Over time, you gradually own less and less of your home but you receive a steady income from it. We'll discuss this further on when we explore retirement income strategies.

CONSIDER DEBT MANAGEMENT
AS A FOOTBALL GAME

If you're a football fan, this example might register. Picture your personal finances as a lifelong football game. Your assets are like gained yards that take you closer to the goal line. Bad debts can be like lost yards, whether through a quarterback sack or a penalty flag that puts you further back and possibly worse off than when you began the football game. Can you score a touchdown?

It stands to reason that if you're burdened with a debt or hefty monthly financing fees to pay, these things will eat up a good portion of your budget, making it harder for you to put that money to better use; kind of like being tackled behind the line of scrimmage or fumbling the ball. Keep trying to advance down the field by using debt or leverage wisely and effectively, where it will help build your net worth and bring you closer to the goal line.

DON'T LET SENTIMENTALITY MUDDY YOUR THINKING

Middle-class millionaires are generally disciplined and responsible enough to avoid taking on high-interest debt. They try to use debt as a tool to benefit from appreciating assets, managing the right side of the balance sheet as much as the left side of the balance sheet (the assets). A few years ago, we had a client who was paying 5 percent interest on a $100,000 mortgage. Meanwhile, she had a $100,000, six-month recurring certificate of deposit (CD) that earned 1 percent annually.

I recommended that if she and her husband were risk adverse, they should consider cashing in the CD and using the proceeds to pay off their mortgage. Six months later they still owned the CD, so I asked why they didn't pay off their mortgage as I had recommended.

Then I learned that the CD was the proceeds from her

mother's estate, and the wife appreciated receiving a monthly statement that reminded her of her mother. I told her, "I completely understand, but that monthly statement is like a $100,000 tombstone for your mother and it's costing you over $4,000 annually—the difference between 5 percent and 1 percent per year on $100,000—to maintain."

It was an "aha" moment for her. She now had a new way of looking at debt. At our next meeting, she told me she had paid off her mortgage because that's what her mother would have wanted her to do.

WORKING WITH FINANCIAL LEVERAGE

One of the most powerful ways to benefit from effective debt management is through its use as a financial leverage tool that can help you build your wealth. If you borrow money at 3 percent or 4 percent, then your assets should be earning at least that much. If not, you should pay off your liabilities. Otherwise, you're falling back financially and not moving forward or growing your net worth. A classic mistake that many people make is to focus only on growing assets (including non-income-producing assets such as cars or boats), but not focusing on growing their overall net worth. However, it's also important to have some cash or CDs on hand for short-term emergencies or savings goals. It's fine if these assets only earn 1 percent. Their primary purpose is to be there when you need the money so they shouldn't be subjected to any risk.

As an example, consider the strategic choice in recent years to *not* pay off your home mortgage at 3 percent or 4 percent.

Instead of accelerating your mortgage payments with a goal of being mortgage-free sooner, you might decide to use the extra cash flow to help you maximize contributions to your retirement accounts, including your 401(k), 403(b), individual retirement account (IRA), or Roth IRA.

If you've already maximized your retirement account contributions, consider buying a portfolio of dividend-paying stocks with dividend yields of 3 percent to 4 percent. In the worst-case scenario, the dividends pay the interest on the mortgage, and in a better scenario, the portfolio of financially strong dividend-paying companies increases in value as they typically have over long periods of time. Since the 1920s, U.S. stocks have returned about 10 percent per year on average. Roughly 30 percent of that amount, or 3 percent per year, has come from dividend returns and about 70 percent, or 7 percent annually, has come from appreciation.[1]

If you think you can earn more than 3 percent to 4 percent a year in investment returns in long-term investments, then go for it!

GOOD CREDIT HABITS

- Pay bills on time.

- Open new credit accounts only as needed.

- Reduce your debt load whenever you can.

- Recognize if you have a credit card impulse-control problem. In that case, *do leave home without it!*

- Consolidate your debt to help you manage it better or save on interest charges.

- Check your credit report each year.

- Use home equity strategically and wisely—it can be a powerful tool if used with discretion and restraint.

CHAPTER 6
Good Value Hunting

VALUE MATTERS AT ALL INCOME LEVELS

Shopping with an eye toward good value is just good consumerism. It doesn't matter how much disposable income you have. Why squander it? Whatever you spend money on, you can always seek the best value in what you purchase—a car, a house, a family vacation, your kids' college tuition, and even your investment manager. Whatever you do, be smart with your money.

DO YOU REALLY NEED THIS?

When shopping for big-ticket items, you can maintain self-discipline by asking yourself, *"Do I really need this?"* Even ask yourself the basic question of *"Can I afford this?"* Also ask, *"Is this a wise or prudent move?"*

For example, do you really need a luxury vehicle? You work hard and, if you can afford a nicer car, why not indulge yourself a bit? Just remember that you're buying a depreciating asset, and by putting more of your money into something that's declining in value over time, you'll have less money available to invest in assets that can and typically do rise in value over time, such as a diversified investment portfolio.

A TALE OF TWO CARS: PORSCHE 911 VERSUS AUDI A3

Consider the difference between Betty and Barb, who are both in the same income range. Betty drives a gorgeous, head-turning, rubber-burning $90,000 Porsche 911 that costs her $1,000 a month in financing. That's like carrying a mortgage! Meanwhile, Barb is more frugal and practical. She drives a pretty decent but more modest Audi A3, rated in 2018 by *U.S. News & World Report* as the "best luxury small car for the money."

Barb's $30,000 sporty, upscale, but more fuel-efficient and modest car gives her all the comfort she really needs, and her five-year $20,000 car loan (after her trade-in and some cash on purchase) is only costing her $375 a month in payments. On top of the $625 a month she's saving (compared to Betty) on her car payments, her insurance is about $90 a month less and her gas expenditures are roughly 35 percent less, saving her another $60 a month.

Tally it up and Barb's saving about $775 a month in car financing, insurance, and gas while still driving a pretty decent vehicle. Now, who would you say is getting the better value for their money? What would you do with that extra $775 a month? Would you save more for retirement, or for your kids' college, or travel more? Maybe you'd do all of the above.

MONTHLY COSTS:
PORSCHE 911 VERSUS AUDI A3

	LONG-TERM CONCERNS	INSURANCE	GAS	TOTAL MONTHLY COST
PORSCHE 911	$1,000	$220	$179	$1399
AUDI A3	$375	$131	$116	$622
MONTHLY SAVINGS	$625	$89	$63	$777

Costs are based on monthly averages. Insurance source: https://www.cheapcarinsurance.net. Gas based on 15,000 miles/year: premium gas at $3 a gallon for the Porsche, regular unleaded at $2.50 for the Audi. Porsche 911 fuel economy: 21 mpg; Audi A3 fuel economy: 29 mpg.[1]

SMART CAR SHOPPING IDEAS

When it comes to actually shopping for any vehicle make and model, you can get better value by following a few good consumer practices:

Pay with cash if you can. Rather than make loan payments each month, try to get ahead of the curve by saving in advance for your next vehicle.

Do your research. Know the car model, features, and accessories that you really want. Use consumer reports and car value websites to find out the fair consumer price range for each vehicle model and year.

Don't succumb to heavy sales pressure; avoid impulse purchases. It helps if you do your research and clearly establish what you want and need.

Use smart timing. Buy at the end of the month, at the end of the model year, or buy on December 31st because most salesmen and dealers have quotas. Dealers have to pay carrying costs for cars held in inventory at the end of the month and year.

Buy last year's model. Once you decide what you want, consider buying a used model from the previous year with as few miles as possible. I've bought many cars with less than 10,000 miles that are up to 30 percent less expensive than a new car. This is particularly effective with high-end vehicles like BMW and Lexus models versus a Honda Accord or Toyota Camry.

SMART HOME PURCHASING POINTERS

There are a number of ways you can get the best deal possible on a house or save money in the long run. One is simply to stay in your house longer…

Buy and move as little as possible. One of the biggest costs of home ownership is the cost of moving. With the understanding that costs vary state by state, consider the following scenario. If you buy a house on Monday and sell it on Tuesday, you'll pay real estate broker commissions of up to 6 percent; real estate transfer taxes (1 to 2 percent); a mortgage appraisal fee ($400); an inspection fee ($400); title fees ($750); title insurance ($500);

and a loan origination fee ($1,000). On a $500,000 home, that's a $30,000 commission plus another $7,500 in transfer tax and an additional $3,000 on the miscellaneous costs I just mentioned. Let's add in the actual cost of the physical move, which would be maybe another $5,000. What are we up to? $45,000 on a $500,000 home, or roughly 9 percent.

You can clearly save some substantial money by buying/selling/moving as infrequently as possible. A good rule of thumb is to buy a house with the expectation to live in it for at least five years. Otherwise, you're probably better off renting. My wife and I bought a small townhouse when we were first married, moved to a modest single-family house with our first child a few years later, and after six years we built our current family home where we've lived for the past 18 years. We even expect to stay in this home for a good while longer.

Buy just what you need. Don't overreach, which can lead to financial pressures. Consider what will resell fairly easily. Imagine trying to sell a $2 million home and having to settle for $300,000 less than you'd like after having it on the market for way too long.

Location. Location. Location. Look for the smallest home in the nicest neighborhood rather than the nicest home in a so-so neighborhood.

Avoid private mortgage insurance. That means not buying a house unless you can put 20 percent of the sales price on a down payment. Otherwise, you're just giving money away. (See: "Buy just what you need.")

Weigh a 15-year versus 30-year mortgage. Which payoff term makes more sense for you? You might take a 30-year mortgage and then accelerate your equity building by making an extra payment per year or adding something to the monthly principal payoff amount when you can. While that will help you own your home outright sooner and save on overall interest rate charges over the life of the loan, there's a trade-off.

For example, if you're paying a 4.5 percent interest rate on your 30-year mortgage, you might earn close to double that by investing in a diversified stock mutual fund in your retirement account. Here's another way to look at it: If you buy dividend-paying stocks that earn a steady dividend equal to your mortgage interest, your investment will help you grow your liquid assets while potentially appreciating in price over the long term. You can always use the dividends to make extra cash mortgage payments, but this flexibility also helps you manage through emergencies or home improvements without being "house poor."

SECOND THOUGHTS ON A SECOND HOME

I see people eager to buy a second home, but with it comes a second mortgage, another layer of real estate tax payments, another set of condo fees, more property insurance payments, more utility bills, and an entire second home that requires repairs.

Do you want to tie up equity in a second home that will only grow as fast as the property can appreciate? Instead of that, smart middle-class millionaires rent vacation homes and keep their options open and their money invested. They might relax by the ocean one year, hike in the mountains the next year, and enjoy quiet time in a cottage by a lake the year after that. By doing this, they pay for only the time they use each property, and don't have the headache of maintenance or guilt if they don't use the second home enough. Not only is it a more carefree way to enjoy a vacation, but they can enjoy checking their investments from the beach and celebrate a good day in the market by treating their family to a nice dinner out!

MAKE COLLEGE MORE AFFORDABLE

Getting a deal on your children's college education can come in a variety of ways, but if you're looking for the biggest bang for your buck, it's hard to beat the discount you'll get by sending your child to an in-state public college.

I point out to our clients that Maryland's in-state tuition only accounts for about one-third of the actual cost of a college education. Another third is covered by state taxes, and a final third is covered by endowments. Therefore, Maryland colleges and universities have some of the lowest in-state tuition rates.

All things being equal, students and parents should take advantage of local community colleges and state universities. Why not give your children limitations as to where and when they can go to school? Letting your child go anywhere they want could cause you to go into debt or delay retirement. In the long run, that may not really be much of a gift to your children. Instead, why not teach your child that we all have limitations? The lesson is that we need to manage around these limitations and constraints to meet our goals and objectives. That's a real life skill.

The goal here is to get your children an education that will help them to become a productive member of society. Once your child understands the constraints, he or she will be more likely to succeed at college or may learn that college isn't right for them and perhaps a training or certification program would be their key to a career. The job market expectations are rapidly changing and parents can save themselves time and money by setting goals and requirements to continue financial support. After all, your child's attitude about his or her education is 90 percent of the success.

I discuss more detailed concerns about paying for college education in Chapter 8: Scaling the Rising Costs of Higher Education.

INVESTMENT ADVICE: WORK WITH A PRO AND MAKE SURE YOUR INTERESTS ALIGN

The first question when it comes to investments is whether to be a do-it-yourselfer or work with a professional investment advisor. The famously fee-conscious people at Vanguard Investments estimate that a competent financial advisor can add roughly 3 percent per year to your net returns.

This makes sense in a number of ways. It's so easy to make costly mistakes with your investments, and the consequences of those mistakes can be enormous.

I often use the example of the house that my wife designed and we built together. We could have gone to the county clerk's office and gotten our permits, gone to Home Depot to buy the two-by-fours, and hired a plumber, an electrician, et cetera. Instead, we hired an experienced professional homebuilder to take care of it all. He had built more than 100 homes before we had built our first.

When we showed the' builder our plans (drawn on graph paper), he said, "This looks great, but you need to move the stairwell to make the house structure sound. You need to think about small details, like where does the light switch go? Most times it's next to the door as you enter and exit a room."

Lastly, when the house was being built there was a problem with the plumbing. I didn't realize it because I'd never built a house before, but the builder did and he told the plumber, "Correct the Kendalls' plumbing problem if you want to work on my next 50 homes." He, and other professional homebuilders, have the experience and buying power that the one-time homebuilder simply does not have.

The same holds true for the do-it-yourself financial homebuilders. They go to a do-it-yourself website, answer a few questions, and receive an asset allocation model that will vary widely depending upon the questions asked and the way you answer. Some examples of questions the do-it-yourself website may ask are: will the individual have a pension? Can they take a lump sum? Do they have charitable desires? What should their risk tolerance be (everyone has higher risk tolerance in bull markets and low risk tolerance in bear markets)? So, even with something as fundamental as that, depending on the website or investment firm, the online financial advisors might have an entirely different asset allocation blueprint that's supposedly tailored to them, but it actually reflects the built-in biases of each investment firm's risk-assessment model. I have seen many websites and investment firms default back to the 60/40 asset allocation based on "the prudent man rule" (what a reasonable person would do in the circumstance).

Thus, as Vanguard has found, a competent financial advisor can add 3 percent per year in value for various reasons such as putting together a structurally sound financial plan that will withstand the test of time, and stop you from potentially making costly mistakes as a do-it-yourselfer.

Once you decide to use a financial advisor, how do you get the best value? Be sure you work with a fee-only fiduciary investment advisor whose financial interests are aligned with yours. When an investment advisor is a fiduciary, he or she has a legal and ethical responsibility to always put the interests of his or her clients at the forefront of their actions. I strongly believe investment advisors should be fiduciaries. This means they sit on the same side of the table as their clients. On the other hand, when an advisor works for a sales commission, his or her interests are often not aligned with helping you and your needs. Instead, it's about making a sale and earning a commission.

Other ways to get value from your investments include:

Avoid trading frequently. The more you trade, the more you'll incur transaction costs, and the greater your potential tax liabilities.

Use index funds and exchange-traded funds. Be mindful of annual expenses. When reviewing potential investments, look at their expense ratios and strongly consider using index funds, which try to replicate a benchmark index rather than outperform it. Because of that, their expenses can be and should be extremely low because they do almost no trading and have little need for individual stock research, and incur next to no tax consequences from gains or losses.

Invest in no-load funds. If you wish to invest in an actively managed mutual fund rather than an index fund, you can buy no-load funds, rather than pay possibly 5 percent or more in a sales load. Sales loads are used to compensate an advisor intent on a buy-and-hold strategy. However, they don't necessarily lead to better investment performance. In fact, it's your money that you're not putting to work for you.

Invest with tax-efficiency in mind. Your investment advisor and accountant can help guide you on how to manage your investments in order to reduce your tax liabilities. One simple step is to review your investment gains toward the end of the year and—if you face possible capital gains taxes—you might look for investments to sell for a loss to offset those tax liabilities. If you have a net capital gains loss, you can use that (up to $3,000 per year) to offset your overall taxable income and carry forward additional losses to take in future years. This can also ease the emotional aspect of selling when a stock is down. Again, working with professionals rather than trying to do financial maneuvers on your own can be worthwhile.

GENERAL SMART FINANCIAL CONSUMER TIPS

- Shop around.

- Consider consignment sales.

- Shop off season.

- Don't impulse purchase. Apply a 48-hour rule on major purchases. (Wait two days or longer before making the purchase.)

- Avoid late-payment fees.

- Review your monthly subscriptions periodically and eliminate unused or underused services.

- Hire professionals who have an incentive to keep you as a long-term client so their advice will be aligned with your goals.

CHAPTER 7

Prudent Ways to Protect Yourself

Risks exist everywhere. If you had a stroke or heart attack, how would you earn a living? What if…

- Your spouse was diagnosed with a terminal illness?

- Your home was robbed?

- You had a serious car accident?

Having the right amount and right type of insurance is paramount, but one size doesn't fit all. How should you evaluate your insurance coverage? A good rule of thumb is that you should insure against potential losses if you don't have enough liquid assets to cover those losses.

Although, you don't need to insure every appliance you own. For example, if your $50 coffee maker stops working, you would simply buy a new one. If your lawn mower needed repair and it turned out the cost was too high, you'd replace it with a new one, cash out of pocket. No problem.

Now let's look at a few key areas where you do need to protect yourself, or at least should consider it.

DO YOUR HOME AND VEHICLE REQUIRE COVERAGE?

Homeowners insurance isn't legally required unless you finance your home with a mortgage. Most mortgage lenders will require insurance.

Vehicle insurance is mandatory in almost every state, but each state has its own laws and regulations about the minimum level of auto insurance protection that you need to carry to cover damages and injuries to others if you're at fault in an accident. Check with your state, and make sure you have at least the required minimum coverage.

Beyond that, as far as covering your own vehicle, ask yourself, "If I total my car and need to buy a replacement, would I face financial hardship in the short term?" If so, then you should have collision insurance.

Next: How high of a deductible should you have on your car? Ask yourself again, what would cause you financial hardship? Could you easily pay $500, $1,000, or $2,000 of repairs bills? If so, consider setting your deductible at your financial hardship pain point. The same is true for your homeowner's insurance policy.

Of course, behind this thinking is the higher your deductible, the lower your insurance premium. As long as you're covering the legally required minimum, why pay for coverage you don't really need?

If you have a lot of risk exposure, consider buying an

umbrella policy that will cover larger claims not normally covered under a standard auto or homeowners policy. They are typically issued in amounts of $1 million, $5 million, and $10 million. Middle-class millionaires will often think of the umbrella policy as their first line of defense. This means that if someone sues you for any reason, such as for wrongful death or debilitating injury accidentally caused by you or a family member, the umbrella insurance company will defend you for the amount of your policy.

HEALTH INSURANCE CAN BE COSTLY, BUT DON'T OVERLOOK HSAS

Health insurance can be costly and it can be confusing to know how much insurance coverage to purchase. As with home and auto coverage, know what your pain point is in terms of what you feel you could pay for and insure beyond that point.

Middle-class millionaires generally take advantage of their employer's health insurance plans. One of the smartest strategies I see time and again is taking advantage of health savings accounts (HSAs). These are pre-tax savings accounts in which your savings accumulate tax-free, and, best of all, distributions can be tax-free as well. That's even better than a Roth IRA because both the contributions and withdrawals are pre-tax. To qualify for an HSA, you have to be covered by an HSA-qualified, high-deductible health insurance plan. To open an account, select from a variety of service providers that offer them, and then select from a list of mutual funds for the bulk of your account. Think of it as a "healthcare IRA" that is mostly invested but also has some cash balance and a debit card to pay for out-of-pocket expenses. It's very convenient and some employees may contribute as well! To learn more, research HSA report cards online and compare which HSA administrators offer the best services and advice to benefit your needs.

DISABILITY INSURANCE: WHAT IF…?

One in four 20-year-olds will become disabled before retirement age, according to the Social Security Administration. What are the risks of not having disability insurance? Everyone's situation is different, but if you are raising a family, ask yourself how your financial obligations would be met if you couldn't work.

If you don't have sufficient capital to cover that risk, you should buy disability and/or life insurance to meet those obligations. This is especially important if you are your family's sole income earner. If you buy this type of insurance, be sure you understand what percentage of your income will be replaced, and whether benefits will be taxable and how long the benefits would last. If your employer offers these benefits, be sure to evaluate those options as they'll likely cost less than purchasing your own policy.

LIFE INSURANCE: DO YOU NEED IT?

Do you need life insurance? At different points in your life, that answer most likely will change. Typically, term insurance can be vital while raising a family. The premiums are much lower than for a whole life or permanent policy because the chances of dying while you're younger are much lower. That being said, ask yourself how your spouse would manage to not only cover your family's living expenses, but also goals like sending your children to college. Typically, a 20- or 30-year term policy covers this timeframe and a financial planner or insurance broker can help you figure out how much of a death benefit you should buy.

Permanent insurance, such as a whole-life or a variable universal life policy, may not be appealing because of its higher premium, and it may not be needed by or recommended for many people. A married couple's first $11 million in assets are free of estate tax. If you're considering life insurance as an optional savings vehicle and if you're a disciplined saver, you might consider separating your insurance needs from your investment vehicle.

Instead of buying a whole-life policy, you'd buy term insurance for the period when your life insurance needs are greatest. Typically, that's while raising a family. Once your family is less dependent on your income—for example, once your kids are out of high school—you could discontinue your term policy. Meanwhile, all along you could be investing the money you save from paying much lower term insurance premiums. This bit of popular financial planning advice is succinctly referred to as "buy term and invest the rest."

With that in mind, however, if you have substantial assets (more than $11 million) or a complex estate, a life insurance policy owned by a trust—through an irrevocable life insurance trust (ILIT)—could lower your estate tax liability and improve your family's cash flow upon death.

I think of life insurance as the amount of money needed to replace your financial commitments after you die. A single person with no children or financial commitments needs no life insurance except possibly a small policy to cover expected burial expenses and provide liquidity while their estate is settled, if no other funds are available.

Often, I sit across the table from a client and ask what happens if Mr. Smith dies tomorrow. If retired, we ask whether Mr. Smith's pension would change. In other words, what is the surviving spouse's benefit? Next, we estimate whether and how much her Social Security benefits would change. Typically, less Social Security comes to the household as Mrs. Smith would no longer receive her benefit, assuming Mr. Smith's is higher. We estimate her expenses without Mr. Smith here. For example, she might not have to pay for the country club membership, the boat slip, or the bar bill, et cetera.

Then we review the assets that Mr. and Mrs. Smith own together and how best for Mrs. Smith to meet her new set of expenses without her husband. If we are short of assets for Mrs. Smith, we recommend they purchase insurance on Mr. Smith's life.

One time we went through this exercise and determined that Mr. Smith's current life insurance policy was no longer needed because the couple had sufficient assets to meet their current and future needs even if Mr. Smith were to die. Their life insurance policy was a term policy and it was about to renew with dramatic premium increases. Because of our assessment, they chose not to renew, and even though Mr. Smith died six months later, Mrs. Smith continues to live comfortably to this day, 10 years later.

LONG-TERM CARE INSURANCE:
SHOULD YOU SELF-INSURE?

Discussions about long-term care insurance often evaluate the need to protect your life savings from being drained in the event you need help—whether at home or in a nursing home—while you live out your older years. But there's an equally valid option to insurance, which is self-insuring. If you choose to self-insure, know what the risks and costs are.

I believe my opinion is in a minority regarding long-term insurance. I really believe the best thing we can do is to help clients create enough overall wealth that they can self-insure against the risk of needing long-term care in the future.

In client seminars, I point out that for a 65-year-old couple today there's a roughly 50 percent chance that one of the two individuals will live to see their 90th birthday.[1] The Social Security Administration's data shows that the 10 percent highest income earners live an average of seven years longer than the 10 percent lowest income earners. The good news is that there's a fair chance you'll live longer than the average American. The flip side of that is there's a better-than-average chance that you'll wind up in a nursing home or need some kind of additional care as you age.

So, what could it cost you? Long-term nursing home costs in the Washington, D.C. area average about $100,000 per year for a private room and just over $90,000 for a semi-private room. There is a 30 percent chance that an individual will need long-term care, but the average person only stays 24 months. Of that 30 percent, fewer than one in 10 will stay in a nursing home longer than five years. That means that only 3 percent of all individuals will need more than five years of nursing home care.

Put all of that together, and I have 97 percent confidence that $500,000 worth of dedicated assets is enough to self-insure for long-term care. There's even a good chance you'll need much less.

If you're an elderly single with high-valued real estate, you could take care of that by selling your family home and investing the capital from your home sale. The proceeds from your home could generate much of the income needed to pay for nursing home care. Meanwhile, you'd no longer have to pay thousands and thousands of dollars on expensive real estate taxes, maintenance, utilities, and other annual home costs.

For example, let's assume you pay property taxes of $10,000; annual home maintenance and miscellaneous home costs of close to $5,000; plus another $3,000 on utilities. Even with your mortgage fully paid off, you'd still have $18,000 in annual carrying costs on your home. That's perhaps one quarter of the annual cost of a semi-private room in a nursing home.

Contrast that with selling a $500,000 home and investing the proceeds at a 3 percent to 5 percent annual return, which would generate $15,000 to $25,000 in annual income. You can understand why some people would prefer to eliminate $18,000 a year in home-related costs along with the associated worries about rising real estate taxes, home maintenance, utilities, and repairs, and instead earn that amount or more from the invested assets.

This may be an outside-the-box concept, but it has helped many people safely enjoy the last years of their lives.

CHAPTER 8
Scaling the Rising Costs of Higher Education

B efore discussing how best to pay for college or university, I'd like to emphasize that giving your children an education is one of the most valuable gifts you can give them. It has much more value than a large estate.

Think of the famous quote, "Give a man a fish, and you feed him for a day. Teach a man to fish, and you feed him for a lifetime."

The gift is preparing your children for a lifetime of success rather than feeding them for a day.

Think of the reason we're sending our children to college: to learn skills and talents that will give them the ability to follow their passions and to be valuable contributors to the greater community. Sure, it's great if your son or daughter wants to go to college to be a left-handed piccolo player, but they should have a clear exit plan after graduation as to what they're going to do with a left-handed piccolo degree.

I've told my children that if they don't know what their college degree will be, they should major in accounting and English. Why? Because as long as they can read and write and know where and how money comes and goes, they will have valuable skills and talents allowing them to do anything once they graduate. So far, my first three children have chosen medicine and engineering as their majors, but I still have a chance with my youngest!

Now, on to how to pay for that preparation to becoming a contributing member of the community...

A FEW KEY ACTIONS

College costs can be daunting, but a few key actions can go a long way.

Attending an in-state public university or a community college can be a major cost-saver if that path is appropriate for your child.

Begin saving when your son or daughter is an infant, and then save steadily so that you can take full advantage of time and compounding investment returns. By starting when the goal is further away, you can invest more aggressively and potentially generate higher returns.

Reduce your costs by sharing them with your child.
Don't neglect other vital investment goals, such as your own retirement fund, while working toward making college more affordable.

THE VALUE OF AN IN-STATE PUBLIC COLLEGE

Picking up from my discussion in Chapter 6: Good Value Hunting, having your child attend an in-state public college or university is one of the best deals you'll ever find. Let's compare the cost of a four-year degree.

A year's tuition and fees at an in-state public college averages just under $10,000 these days, according to the College Board website. Add another $10,000 or so for room and board, and the annual cost is $20,770. (See details in the table below.) Multiply by four and add a conservative 3 percent annual inflation rate, and the combined total cost of a bachelor's degree for a student who entered college in September 2017 would be almost $87,000.

CURRENT COSTS OF DIFFERENT FORMS OF HIGHER EDUCATION[1]

	PUBLIC 2-YEAR COMMUNITY COLLEGE	PUBLIC 4-YEAR IN-STATE COLLEGE	PRIVATE 4-YEAR COLLEGE
TUITION & FEES	$3,570	$9,970	$34,740
ROOM & BOARD	$8,400	$10,800	$12,210
TUITION & FEES + ROOM & BOARD	$11,970	$20,770	$46,950
4-YEAR COST INCLUDING 3% INFLATION WITH 2-YEAR COLLEGE SWITCHING TO 4-YEAR PROGRAM	$69,030	$86,894	$196,421

Compare that with the price tag of a four-year private university: $34,740 in tuition plus $12,210 for room and board in the 2017–2018 academic year, for a total cost of $46,950 in year one. Apply 3 percent inflation and add three years for a total price tag of $196,421 for a bachelor's degree. Ask yourself if the additional $110,000 is worth it.

I know what I would do and what many smart middle-class millionaires have done. Why burden yourself or your child with an extra $100,000 or more in debt? How much more debt will you be looking at for a master's degree or a PhD?

You can make a bachelor's degree even more affordable. Consider having your student attend a community college for two years and then transfer, applying those credits to a four-year state college or university (if that college will accept the community college credits). Because the average annual cost at a community college is roughly half that of a public university, you could save about $18,000 in those first two years. That cuts the $87,000 total cost down to about $69,000 on average. That's quite a savings from the $196,000 estimated cost of a private university.

Also, by sparing your kids from a lot of unnecessary student loan debt, you'll give them a head start toward becoming middle-class millionaires themselves.

START SAVING EARLY

No matter which route you choose, you'll still have a large amount to save. Here are some ways to make that saving as easy and painless as possible:

Start saving for your children's college the day your child is born. Like saving for your retirement, the sooner you get started, the longer your savings can grow, and the easier it will be to save a substantial amount of tuition costs. Let's assume an $87,000 total price tag for a four-year in-state university degree. If you were saving for a public in-state tuition for newborn twins, factor in 3 percent annual inflation over two decades and that $174,000 combined tuition would be more like $296,000.

Assuming you split the costs down the middle with your kids, you'd have to pick up $148,000 of the tab. If you start saving the day they're born, you could hit that $148,000 target by saving $270 a month and investing it aggressively enough so that it grows at a hypothetical 7 percent annually for the 22 years until they graduate.[2]

Let's say you delay saving until they're out of diapers and daycare. If you simply wait five years and then make the same $270 monthly contributions, you'd fall $60,000 short. To hit your $148,000 goal in 13 years based on the same assumptions of 3 percent inflation on college costs and 7 percent earnings per year, you'd need to raise your monthly savings to $427.

Now, what if you waited until they entered high school to start saving? First, you'd have to lower your expected rate of return to 5 percent because you'd have to invest somewhat more conservatively. Based on the initial assumptions of $270 a month savings and 3 percent annual tuition inflation, you'd fall $122,000 short of your target. To make that target in just four years, you'd have to bump up monthly savings to $1,172. Clearly, it's much easier if you start saving long before your first conversation with your kids about the value of a college education!

Split the cost four ways. Another way to carve out costs is to use four sources. First is your college savings account. After saving a nice sum, you can draw it down steadily to pay for one-quarter of their total college costs. Next, pay some of the bills with current cash flow. This should be doable because you won't be adding to their college savings account by then. Instead, just earmark that cash for current bills.

Then, your child can be responsible for the other two slices of the cost. One portion can come from a federal student loan that your child can sign up for through the Free Application for Federal Student Aid (FAFSA) program (visit https://studentaid.ed.gov to learn more about federal student loans). Your child will eventually pay back that debt, and they can pay for the final portion with earnings from a summer job and part-time work during the school year. In addition to making the costs more manageable, this is a great way to teach your child responsibility. I believe children are more likely to value their education if they have to contribute toward it financially. It means they have some skin in the game.

WHICH COLLEGE ACCOUNT TO USE?

529 plans: How would you like to save for college? In the most popular designated college savings plan, the 529 college plan, you invest after-tax money that grows tax-free, and you pay no tax on the funds and any investment gains if you use the proceeds for "qualified educational expenses," which can include tuition, books, and room and board.

There are actually two types of 529 college plans:

1. A prepaid college tuition plan that lets you lock in future tuition at today's costs.

2. The investment plan in which you typically invest in an age-based allocation, which is adjusted gradually to a more conservative mix as the beneficiary approaches college age.

On top of the investment's tax-free growth and withdrawals, many states including Maryland offer an additional incentive to encourage state residents to use their home state's 529 plan. You can get an annual state income tax deduction of up to $2,500 per account by contributing to a Maryland Prepaid College Trust, and another in the Maryland College Investment Plan. In other words, you can deduct up to $5,000 per child on your state income tax return. If you're married, that doubles to $10,000. If you contribute more than $2,500 to either account in any year, you can apply the excess amount to future tax years.

There are a couple of additional benefits to using a 529 plan account. If you are the account holder, there will be minimal impact on how much student aid your child can apply for. Also, you can change the account beneficiary at any point; for example, if your child doesn't attend college or graduates with an account balance remaining. 529 plans can also be a great tax-efficient way for the student's grandparents to help manage their estate. That's because their contributions count toward their annual gift tax exclusion, currently $15,000 per recipient.

There are a variety of other college savings options, but I don't think any other savings options can match 529 plans for their multitude of benefits. Briefly, they include:

Roth IRAs: You can use Roth individual retirement accounts as a combined retirement savings and college savings vehicle. Your after-tax contributions will grow tax-free and withdrawals won't be taxed if used for qualified educational expenses. If you don't use it for any college costs, the money can continue to grow until you withdraw it in retirement.

Custodial college accounts: A couple of these traditional custodial plans—Uniform Gifts to Minors Act (UGMA) and Uniform Transfers to Minors Act (UTMA)—have become less popular since 529 plans came along, but they can still serve a purpose. Unlike 529 plans, the assets in UTMAs and UGMAs belong to the beneficiary, who can use them for anything—educational or other—once they reach the "age of trust termination," typically 18 or 21.

That aspect can be a plus if your goal is simply to give your children money to do with what they choose, but it could be a drawback if you have a strong desire to encourage and help pay for college enrollment. Also, note that as an asset belonging to the child, custodial accounts will factor more heavily in financial aid eligibility.

Coverdell Education Savings Accounts (ESAs): These accounts are like a 529-lite with tax-free qualified withdrawals, but the contribution limit is just $2,000 per year. One unique plus is that you can use Coverdell accounts for any educational expenses, from kindergarten through 12th grade, as well as for college costs.

HOW TO INVEST YOUR COLLEGE SAVINGS

The general approach to asset allocation for college accounts is to gradually and steadily scale back exposure to risk from age five and under (when you can have most of your savings in stocks) to the college years (when you'll want more assets in bonds and cash). Of course, it depends how risk-tolerant you are as an investor. Basically, start off investing as aggressively as you feel you can and then scale back gradually.

After all, you'll want to at least keep pace with rising college costs, but not risk being hurt by a market downturn when you don't have enough time to make up your losses. Below is a table that provides some suggestions for asset allocation based on risk comfort and age of the child.

A SAMPLE ASSET ALLOCATION
GRID FOR COLLEGE SAVINGS

CHILD'S AGE	CONSERVATIVE	MODERATE	AGGRESSIVE
5 and younger	50% stocks/ 50% bonds	80% stocks/ 20% bonds	100% stocks
10	25% stocks/ 75% bonds	60% stocks/ 40% bonds	75% stocks/ 25% bonds

Continued on Next Page

CHILD'S AGE	CONSERVATIVE	MODERATE	AGGRESSIVE
15	25% stocks/ 50% bonds/ 25% cash	40% stocks/ 60% bonds	50% stocks/ 50% bonds
College age	100% cash	10% stocks/ 60% bonds/ 30% cash	25% stocks/ 50% bonds/ 25% cash

Source: Based on asset allocation from collegeadvantage.com as indicated in
https://ptmoney.com/suggested-asset-allocation-for-your-529-plan,
and modified to reflect more aggressive T. Rowe Price asset allocation
in the Maryland 529 plan at https://maryland529.com.

The easiest and perhaps best thing is to follow the age-based allocations that your 529 plan can provide as a default.

STAY BALANCED IN YOUR PRIORITIES

Here are a few final reminders or thoughts on college savings.

First, don't shortchange your own retirement savings by putting too much of your available savings into your kids' college accounts and not enough into your retirement plan. As noted earlier, there are some great ways that you can substantially reduce your college payment obligations and not hurt the quality of your kids' college experiences, such as looking at in-state public colleges and sharing the cost with your college-age kids.

You shouldn't have to radically diverge from what should be steady career-long retirement savings habits. Retirement savings should *always* be your top investment focus. Juggle your priorities, but don't forego your regular retirement plan contributions.

Second, don't feel compelled to use your 529 plan account proceeds if you don't really need to. For example, if you can find other ways to pay as you go, by leaving assets in your 529 plan you'll leave yourself the option of using them elsewhere. Perhaps let them keep accumulating value and apply them to your grandkids' college payments.

Finally, if you are willing to pay taxes on the 529 account earnings plus a 10 percent penalty, you could use them for your retirement. Better yet, you could hedge some of your bets on retirement savings and college savings by putting some money into a Roth IRA that you designate as an either-or-both account. It could complement your 529 plan and provide some flexibility in how you use it down the road.

CHAPTER 9

Take Advantage of All Savings Vehicles

To save effectively for your future, besides saving enough and investing appropriately, you also have to choose the best or most appropriate savings vehicles for your needs. The key differentiator is how your money is taxed.

Don't let the alphabet soup of account types, numbers, names, and abbreviations—401(k), 403(b), 457, 529, IRA, TSP, HSA, Roth, et cetera—put you off.

Instead of trying to memorize all of that, focus on the major tax distinctions. There are three basic categories of accounts:

	CONTRIBUTIONS	WITHDRAWALS
TAXABLE ACCOUNTS	No special tax treatment	No special tax treatment
TRADITIONAL PRE-TAX / TAX-DEFERRED ACCOUNTS	Contributions made with pre-tax dollars, meaning you get the tax break today	Account distributions are taxable

Continued on Next Page

Continued from Previous Page

	CONTRIBUTIONS	WITHDRAWALS
ROTH AFTER-TAX / TAX-FREE ACCOUNTS	Contributions made with after-tax dollars—meaning you don't take a tax break today	Distributions are tax-free after age 59½ if the account has been open at least 5 years. 100% of contributions can be withdrawn tax free at any time. Many exceptions exist for penalty-free withdrawal of earnings before age 59½.

Some other accounts with slightly different tax treatments are described below.

First are *taxable accounts*, where you save or invest with after-tax dollars, and there's no special tax treatment. This means that annual earnings—including dividends and capital gains—are taxable, but you don't automatically pay a tax when you withdraw or take distributions from the account other than if you sell an investment for a capital gain.

Designated retirement accounts can be either "*traditional*" *pre-tax accounts* or "*Roth*" *accounts*, which are made with after-tax dollars. They come in a variety of names, but the key question in choosing one or the other is, "Are you better off investing on a pre-tax or after-tax basis?"

Other accounts you can use may be *tax-deferred accounts with pre-tax contributions*. The two basic types are tax-deferred individual retirement accounts (IRAs) and tax-deferred employer-sponsored workplace savings plans. Workplace plans include 401(k) and 403(b) plans, thrift savings plans (TSPs), 457(b) plans, SEP plans, and SIMPLE IRAs. 403(b)s are like 401(k)s but are used by nonprofit companies, religious groups, school districts, and governmental organizations, while 457 plans are available to certain state and local government employees. SEP and SIMPLE IRA plans are designed for small businesses and their employees.

These details may seem confusing, but the key is that these traditional (non-Roth) retirement savings plans feature contributions made with pre-tax dollars. That means you receive a tax deduction for the money you contribute up to a certain allowable amount each year. The earnings grow tax-deferred (no taxes are paid while the money is in the account), and then distributions are taxed at your ordinary income tax rate when you withdraw your savings.

Because withdrawals are intended to take place in retirement, you might expect to receive more favorable tax treatment if you think you'll be in a lower tax bracket in retirement. If that's the case, investing in a traditional tax-deferred account would allow you to receive the tax break when working, when your tax rate is higher than you expect it will be in retirement.

Although many people expect that they'll earn less and pay taxes at a lower rate in retirement, that's not always the case. You might be pushed into a higher tax bracket because of taking required minimum distributions (RMDs) or pension distributions. One thing to keep in mind is that we have no idea of future changes to the tax code or what the marginal income tax brackets may be in the future.

Roth accounts with after-tax contributions are an entirely different animal. The tax treatment on Roth IRAs and Roth 401(k), 403(b), and 457(b) plans flips the traditional accounts' tax treatment on its head. Instead of receiving a tax break up front by investing dollars before they are taxed, you invest after-tax dollars. Instead of being taxed on withdrawals, you can make withdrawals completely tax-free. Both traditional and Roth versions of these retirement accounts feature tax-deferred growth of earnings.

A key advantage of a Roth account is that you'll never pay taxes on your earnings as long as you follow certain rules. The contributions are made with money that has already been taxed, so that portion is tax-free when withdrawn no matter what or when. Your earnings will also be tax-free if you don't withdraw them until you're at least age 59½ and the account has been open for five years.

Another great benefit of a Roth IRA is its great flexibility. Once the five-year rule is satisfied, you can access the earnings penalty-free (you only pay ordinary income tax on the earnings) for the purpose of a first-time home purchase or to pay higher education costs for you or your children. If you don't have kids yet, saving in a Roth IRA in your 20s and 30s will create a savings vehicle that you can use for several possible goals. It's also a good "emergency fund" because the earnings are penalty-free if used for medical expenses or disability. This is a good option for young people too if they're laid off and need to pay for COBRA, the health insurance program that can serve as a bridge for coverage between jobs.

Roth IRAs also have a special benefit: Unlike other retirement accounts, you'll never be forced to take required minimum distributions. That means that your money can keep growing tax-free as long as you want, and you can even pass them on to your heirs with no tax consequences.

Roth accounts are most attractive to younger workers who may not be at their peak earnings level and may be in a lower tax bracket. Roth IRAs also can be attractive to older workers (older than age 70½) who are still working, as traditional IRAs are no longer available to them. There's also much more flexibility with Roth IRA withdrawals than traditional IRAs.

I won't describe the eligibility requirements in detail here, but if you qualify to contribute, all workplace retirement accounts allow annual contributions (as of 2018) of $18,500, with another $6,000 if you're 50 or older. IRAs have a $5,500 annual contribution limit, with another $1,000 for those 50 or older.

Two special investing accounts are *529 plans* and *health savings plans*. Up until now, all accounts—other than taxable accounts—that I've mentioned are retirement accounts. There are also a couple of non-retirement accounts that have noteworthy tax-favorable features.

529 college savings plans are funded with after-tax dollars and have much higher contribution limits. Like Roths, they allow for tax-free withdrawals as long as the proceeds are used for eligible college-related expenses, including tuition, fees, computer equipment, and room and board. If you use the withdrawals for a non-eligible purpose, you'll pay a 10 percent penalty and owe taxes on the earnings that you withdraw.

Health Savings Accounts (HSAs) are a rare breed. They actually offer three tax advantages: you contribute with pre-tax dollars (and receive a tax break up front), earnings grow tax-deferred, and distributions are income tax-free as well if used for qualified medical expenses. If any portion of a distribution isn't used for qualified medical expenses, those proceeds will be taxable and subject to a 20 percent penalty. Then, when you turn 65, you can use this type of account for any purpose penalty-free and tax-free.

To illustrate some practical strategies around these different options, consider a young couple I work with who are in the 22 percent marginal income tax bracket. They have two young children. They make pre-tax contributions to their 401(k)s and they contribute a bit to the husband's Roth account and to 529 college savings plans for their kids each year. They also own a rental property that provides additional tax deductions.

Taking all this into account, I've encouraged the husband to balance Roth and pre-tax 401(k) contributions and set up monthly contributions to the 529 accounts. I believe this will provide a better balance between current and future tax benefits. That's a form of tax diversification, which we'll look at more in the next chapter.

That's a lot to keep straight, so in general, focus on the tax treatment that's most beneficial for you and try to strike a balance between enjoying your tax break today and down the road.

CHAPTER 10

Keep Options Open Through Tax Diversification

I n the previous chapter we discussed taking advantage of all savings vehicles, and then reviewed the major types of investment accounts based on their tax benefits. Now let's look more closely at how to use these accounts collectively for the greatest overall strategic benefit. What types of assets should you place in what type of account to optimize their after-tax earnings? What are the benefits of having diversified accounts based on their tax treatment?

BASICS OF TAX DIVERSIFICATION

The point of diversification is to make sure you're not overly concentrated in any one investment. Simply put, it's not having all your eggs in one basket. Because of the different tax treatments for various accounts, it can be advantageous to spread your assets across the three major types of accounts: *taxable*, *tax-deferred*, and *tax-free* accounts. Each type of account offers its own advantages.

Having some of your assets in each bucket can provide you with options and control when you take withdrawals to meet future living expenses, and also avoid being bumped up into a higher tax bracket, when possible.

TAKE ADVANTAGE OF QUALIFIED CHARITABLE DISTRIBUTIONS

To illustrate the benefits of tax diversification and keeping your options open, consider a couple in their mid-70s who have to take required minimum distributions from their individual retirement account (IRA). In their case, they don't need the cash because they live comfortably on Social Security and a pension. This couple donates $10,000 to their church annually. By making the donation from their IRAs, they avoid paying taxes on the donated amount and do not have to itemize their deduction. By doing so, they reduce their current year's taxable income and preserve their joint account assets. This strategy is called a qualified charitable distribution (QCD).

The changes in income tax rules in the Tax Cuts and Jobs Act, the 2017 year-end tax reform bill, make QCDs an important tax-saving strategy. The QCD allows taxpayers to take the full standard deduction—$24,000 per couple plus $1,300 per person over age 65, or $26,600—*plus* they can donate to their church with tax-free money!

WHAT TO DO WITH A ROTH IRA INHERITANCE

Even though a top priority in personal finance is to save diligently for your retirement, situations sometimes arise in which you are able to put money to another good use at a key time in your life so as to get on better financial footing. For example, Bob, age 33, inherits a $250,000 Roth IRA. An inherited Roth IRA has required minimum distributions (RMDs) based on the age of the beneficiary, but they are not taxable. At 33, Bob must take at least $5,000 (roughly 2 percent of the $250,000 balance) out of his account. He could then use that $5,000 to contribute to his own Roth IRA assuming he has earned income, and that money continues to grow tax-free for an additional 50 years.

What would *you* do with $250,000 in sudden wealth? There's no one "right" answer here. Some people might max out their retirement contributions for the next decade or so. Others might use some of the windfall to buy a house if that was a major priority. The takeaway: You need to make your money work for you in the best way for your situation. More tax diversification equals more options, and having a Roth IRA can offer a powerful benefit to you or your heirs, wherever they are in life when they inherit it.

BENEFITS OF TAXABLE ACCOUNTS

While tax-deferred retirement accounts and tax-free Roth retirement accounts offer obvious tax advantages, you can use taxable accounts to lower your taxes as well. Here are some benefits of taxable accounts:

Lower taxes on withdrawals: One key advantage of taxable accounts is that long-term capital gains are taxed at a lower rate than your ordinary income tax rate, which is the tax rate you'll pay on withdrawals from traditional (non-Roth) individual retirement accounts (IRAs) and 401(k)s.

The long-term capital gains tax rate is 0 percent for single filers who have less than $38,600 in taxable income and joint filers who earn up to $77,200. The rate increases to 15 percent for single filers earning up to $425,800, and for joint filers who earn up to $479,000. Keep in mind this is the *long-term capital gains rate*, which applies to assets that you hold onto for more than a year. With a short-term capital gain (held for one year or less), you will pay the higher federal marginal income tax rates:

- 10 percent or 12 percent instead of 0 percent

- 22 percent to 35 percent versus 15 percent

- 37 percent instead of 20 percent

Additionally, if more than $250,000 of the income for married taxpayers filing jointly ($200,000 for single filers) is derived from investments, then a 3.8 percent Medicare tax is added on investment income over these thresholds.

RMDs: One drawback to traditional IRAs and 401(k) account assets is the RMDs, which apply once you reach age 70½. Because only one type of account has this requirement, it can factor into your annual decision of which account to withdraw from and how much money to withdraw from each.

To preserve your traditional IRA/401(k) assets as much as possible, take no more than the required minimum each year. After that you can decide how much to withdraw from your taxable and tax-free accounts to make up the right mix of income and tax liability each year.

Step-up basis: When assets in your taxable account are passed on to your heirs, the beneficiaries will receive more favorable taxation because of a step up on the tax basis. The assets are treated as if purchased by the beneficiaries when they are inherited. The tax basis is stepped up, which means taxes will only be owed on gains that occur after the inheritance.

Harvest your tax losses: One of the great tools you can use to manage your annual income tax liability is tax loss harvesting. As the phrase implies, you can harvest any tax losses if you have some. You realize investment losses by selling underperforming assets in a given year to offset any realized capital gains that would otherwise be taxed. If you don't have realized capital gains or if your realized capital losses exceed your gains, you can apply that capital loss of up to $3,000 a year to offset your ordinary income. If you have a net loss of more than $3,000, you can carry over the remaining amount and use it in future tax years. Also keep in mind the wash sale rule if you sell an investment while it is down to take advantage of the tax loss.

You must wait at least 31 days before repurchasing that same investment.

DONOR-ADVISED FUNDS OFFER MANY BENEFITS

Donor advised funds (DAF) are a powerful tax-friendly vehicle for charitable donations. They offer numerous benefits:

- You receive an income tax deduction of the full market value in the year you contribute to your DAF.

- If you gift appreciated assets—such as stocks, bonds, or mutual funds—you avoid paying the capital gains tax you would otherwise pay when you sell the asset.

- Your DAF is not subject to estate taxes.

- Cash not given to a charity can be reinvested in the DAF and grow tax-free.

- If you are subject to alternative minimum tax (AMT), your DAF contribution will lower the AMT you owe.

All of this, *and* you can give to your favorite charity via the DAF. To do this properly when donating appreciated stock, be sure to transfer the stock directly to the DAF without selling the stock.[1] Keep in mind, there's a charitable deduction limit of 30 percent of your AGI, but any unused charitable deductions can be carried forward for up to five years.

ASSET LOCATION

Asset location is the strategic decision to place assets in the type of account where you'll receive the optimal tax treatment and ultimately the best after-tax return. It's a key consideration because certain types of assets are taxed differently than others, as are holdings within certain accounts.

For example, municipal bonds are tax-free in certain circumstances. Accordingly, they make sense to have in a taxable account, and it's typically best to own individual securities in taxable accounts and mutual funds in tax-deferred accounts. This is because mutual funds tend to distribute taxable capital gains at the end of the year whether or not individual investors want those gains.

In a taxable account, you might find yourself paying taxes on a fund's gains even though you haven't benefited from those gains. They're still essentially an unrealized gain (the profit exists only on paper) and yet you owe taxes on it! But some mutual funds are more tax-friendly and might be fine in a taxable account. These include tax-efficient mutual funds, which use various strategies to minimize annual tax obligations, and index funds, which replicate an index and avoid trading or incurring capital gains.

Generally, individual stocks are more favorable in a taxable account because you or your portfolio manager can realize capital gains, which are also taxed at lower rates than ordinary income tax. In contrast, taxable bonds and bond funds make more sense in a retirement account because earnings are taxed at your ordinary tax rate.

Note, however, that many factors can influence where your investments should be located. Your situation and overall asset allocation might be key things to consider.

Also consider that stocks and stock funds tend to outperform bonds and bond funds over the long term as investors are generally compensated with higher returns for taking on more volatility. Accordingly, placing them in a tax-deferred account where their returns can keep compounding could lead to dramatically higher long-term results.

For example, if you contribute $10,000 initially and make annual contributions of $10,000 for the next 30 years compounding at a hypothetical 8 percent annual rate of return, your investment would grow to approximately $1,233,000 after 30 years. On the other hand, a compounded annual rate of 4 percent over the same period would result in approximately $593,000 in savings. The rates of return here are used for illustrative purposes.

This can be especially powerful in a Roth IRA or Roth 401(k) account, where you'll receive your entire balance without any taxes owed as long as you hold the account for at least five years and you are at least 59½ years old.

Thus, you should make your overall investment decision on the merits of the investment itself and not allow the tax tail to wag the investment dog. After selecting an investment, consider the tax implications and where the asset might be best placed. Always consult with a trusted accountant or tax expert if you need guidance on tax matters.

HOW BEST TO BALANCE THE THREE
TYPES OF ACCOUNTS

As noted earlier, it's generally good to have some money in all three types of accounts for maximum diversification. Also, keep in mind these are just general guidelines. Everyone's situation is different.

With those disclaimers out of the way, it can be beneficial to invest in a Roth retirement plan account early in your career when your income is likely lower, along with your tax rate. Many employers now offer Roth as well as pre-tax options for your contributions, so it may be better for you to pay taxes on your retirement savings earlier rather than later in your career, when you will likely be in a higher tax bracket.

Another period that could be appropriate for Roth contributions is late in your career, especially if you're gradually phasing into retirement and possibly working less and earning less money annually.

Admittedly, it can be tough psychologically to decide to contribute to a Roth 401(k) and not claim the immediate tax deduction you get with a traditional pre-tax 401(k) contribution. Additionally, the option to make Roth contributions in retirement plan accounts is a relatively new policy. Accordingly, most people have most of their savings on the pre-tax side. You can split your contributions and contribute to both sides of the tax wall.

To provide a better balance of options in your retirement as you get closer to retiring, you might want to review your respective account balances and consider making Roth contributions to even things up. This is especially true for high-income earners, who have a heavy imbalance in their non-Roth accounts. Because there's more at stake, the potential benefits are greater.

If your income exceeds the contribution eligibility requirement for a Roth IRA, you may want to consider the "backdoor" Roth approach. With a backdoor Roth IRA, you contribute to a non-deductible individual retirement account and then convert that IRA to a Roth IRA account within the same year. Unlike a regular conversion from a traditional IRA, no taxes are owed on the conversion because you contributed to the non-deductible IRA with after-tax dollars. The non-deductible IRA contribution doesn't have income-eligibility limits, but you need to have earned income to make a non-deductible contribution to a traditional IRA. Also, you can only create a backdoor Roth before you reach age 70½.

This is another smart way to rebalance your retirement accounts along with regular conversions from a tax-deductible traditional IRA to a Roth. However, with a conversion, you'll owe taxes because you made your initial IRA contribution with pre-tax (tax-deductible) dollars.

The key in all of this is to balance your tax liabilities in retirement by establishing the ability to make both tax-deferred and tax-free withdrawals, and to reduce your exposure to required minimum distributions (RMDs). In addition to broadening your retirement distribution options later on, you'll allow this money to keep growing tax-free for many years, possibly even beyond your lifetime.

Back in the early 1980s, when 401(k)s were offered as a way to shift the burden of retirement savings from businesses to employees, it was assumed that people would be in a lower tax bracket in retirement simply because they would require less income. However, today we find retirees do not necessarily spend less; they simply spend on different things. We also find that tax brackets can't be accurately predicted. They could rise or fall based on a variety of political and economic issues.

The bottom line is that it's important to create tax diversification and always try to maintain a variety of options. It's like working with a full toolbox, and you maintain control of your taxes at any bracket. All the same, the higher your marginal tax bracket, the more you'll likely benefit from tax diversification and tax management strategies.

CHAPTER 11

Asset Allocation Through the Ages

To watch CNBC or read the financial press, you'd never know what the most important factor in determining your investment returns is. That's how little attention they pay to it. So, what is the most important factor?

It's *not* picking the next dominant, game-changing Apple or Google stock before it skyrockets, because for every Apple or Google, there are 10 other companies that are worth nothing today. The fact is you only hear about the winners.

It's *not* rotating in and out of sectors at just the right time or getting in and out of the stock market at an ideal time. That's called market timing. Very few institutional investors—professionals who manage multi-billion dollar portfolios—have a track record of outperforming the market more than 50 percent of the time.

The most important factor—the key to success in investing—is simply allocating your assets in the optimal way based on your *risk tolerance, time horizon, level of investment knowledge,* and *chances of needing the money sooner than you think.* Of course, it's understandable that asset allocation doesn't get a lot of attention in the daily financial media. After all, it doesn't "sell newspapers" and there's little "news value" in sticking with something that is designed to work consistently over the long term, but isn't full of attractive bells and whistles.

Middle-class millionaires incorporate asset allocation into their decision-making because it's a key aspect of well-laid financial plans. Let's take a look at asset allocation and review some best practices to keep in mind and some common mistakes to try to avoid.

ASSET ALLOCATION 101

Consider this a refresher course or an introduction to asset allocation if you're new to investing. Here are the basics:

Risk gets rewarded: Asset allocation begins with the assumption that investments that tend to be riskier or more volatile also tend to reward investors with higher expected returns (known as a risk premium) to compensate them for taking that additional risk.

Seeking an optimal return: Also, by having a broadly diversified mix of assets that don't all behave the same way in a given situation (low correlation with one another), you can strive to achieve an optimal return for a given level of risk. Consider it the "sweet spot." It's also known as "the efficient frontier" in the modern portfolio theory (MPT), which earned professor Harry Markowitz a Nobel Prize in Economics in 1990.

Tailored to the individual: Where asset allocation really earns its stripes is in recognizing that everyone is different. So, your individualized asset allocation should position you for optimal long-term investment results if it accurately:

> ***Reflects how comfortable you are with risk.*** Some of us simply are more able and willing to take a greater degree of risk in return for higher potential rewards.

> ***Takes into account how long you expect to leave your investment alone.*** That's affected by your investment horizon and how financially secure you are. If there's little chance that you'll touch your investment before your targeted date, you can afford to take higher risk. The longer you can leave your investment untouched, the greater the opportunity that your portfolio could rebound from a downturn, such as the financial crisis of 2008. Think of the contrast between people who needed their money in 2009 and those of us who've benefited from the luxury of time, watching paper losses vanish as stocks rebounded and climbed higher over the past decade.

> ***Considers your investment knowledge level.*** More knowledgeable, better informed, and better read investors tend to be more comfortable with risks and even more aggressive overall in their investment approach. For example, they might be more open to including a modest allocation to alternative investments, such as commodities, real estate, foreign markets, or convertible bonds. These individual investments offer the potential for higher expected rates of return. While they are statistically riskier as individual investments, they offer the benefit of potentially higher returns with lower overall portfolio

risk because their returns or price movements are not highly correlated when used in combination with each other. What is nice about investing in today's market as compared to 20 and 30 years ago is that there is now a plethora of publicly traded mutual funds, exchange-traded funds (ETFs), and securities that give individual investors relatively easy low-cost exposure to these asset classes that were previously very difficult and expensive for middle-class millionaires to have access to.

Key steps: Typically, your asset allocation will involve taking a risk tolerance quiz that helps you and/or your financial advisor determine where you are on a scale from conservative (or very conservative) to moderate to aggressive (or very aggressive). You might find a model portfolio that suggests a typical mix of assets for you as a conservative, moderate, or aggressive investor at a certain life stage.

ASSET ALLOCATION BEST PRACTICES

Focus on your true time horizon. In retirement planning, some people see age 65 as a key date, after which everything changes. It's true that some things will change the day you retire. You'll no longer be accumulating wealth. Instead, you'll be focused on preserving it, but that should affect your asset allocation only marginally at first. Even at age 65, many of us can expect to live another three decades. Because of this, some of your money should be positioned to take advantage of that still lengthy timeframe. (See the discussion on tranches, below.)

Remember, the key is to make sure you don't outlive your

money. In order for your money to last as long as you, it should include a growth component (stocks) that gradually declines well into your retirement. Also, depending on how much wealth you have and how confident you are that you won't outlive your money, your time horizon could extend into the lives of your heirs. If you expect to leave an inheritance, you might invest somewhat more aggressively, knowing your investments have even longer to recover and make up any lost ground.

Maintain short-term and long-term tranches. Here's an effective method that can enable you to take greater risk with part of your portfolio in the quest for higher returns, while also helping you ride through a bear market in retirement and take volatility in stride with minimal impact. You build your portfolio with a focus on tranches or tiers that represent the short, medium, and longer terms.

Although it's easy to forget in a long bull market, stocks sometimes retreat. Without proper precautions, a market crash can potentially be devastating for many people, but you can create a buffer to protect yourself from being forced to sell securities in order to pay for short-term living expenses.

The buffer, or short-term tranche, consists of short-term assets that you use to meet short-term needs. You can use this "cash reserve"—which is focused on preserving your capital—to fund the first six months to two years of your retirement living expenses. The goal is to have a stable source of liquid money in a combination of a bank account, money market fund, short-term CD, and/or a Treasury bill.

A second tranche, intended to generate somewhat higher total return, is used as a steady source of income that you could use for the rest of your first decade of retirement. It could include income-producing fixed income and conservative, high-yielding, blue-chip equity investments. As you periodically need to replenish your short-term tranche, you can transfer money as needed from this medium-term, income-generating tranche.

The third tranche has more of a growth focus because you can afford to leave it alone for a decade or longer. This can be focused on stocks, and is geared for better long-term returns, with the understanding that you can take volatility in stride over the course of a decade or two or longer.

By using this tiered or tranche approach, even if a bear market arrived early in your retirement, your equity holdings would be protected and would have time to recover. This knowledge should reassure you and dissuade you from making impulsive financial decisions, especially when the market is volatile or geopolitical news might make you feel uneasy.

Monitor your asset allocation regularly; rebalance as necessary. You may think of asset allocation as a long-term "set it and forget it" strategy. If so, you're partly right. Asset allocation should be done with a long-term goal, but like any investment strategy, it should be monitored to make sure it remains on track.

Let's look at the long-term growth tranche. This is a subset of your portfolio that you can afford to take greater risk with because you have a high degree of confidence that your other assets and sources of retirement income will pay for your expenses for a decade or so.

With that in mind, you allocate 25 percent each of this tranche in U.S. large-cap stocks (S&P 500 Index), U.S.

small-cap stocks (Russell 2000), international stocks (MSCI EAFE), and REITs (FTSE Nareit Index). Let's see how these four asset classes would have performed for you had you allocated one-quarter of your money in this tranche to each of them in early 2016.

	U.S. LARGE CAP	U.S. SMALL CAP	INTER- NATIONAL STOCKS	REITS	TOTALS
INITIAL ALLOCA- TION 1/1/16	$25,000 (25%)	$25,000 (25%)	$25,000 (25%)	$25,000 (25%)	$100,000 (100%)
2016 RETURNS	12%	21.3%	1.0%	9.3%	
TOTALS 12/31/16	$28,000 (25.25%)	$30,325 (27.34%)	$25,250 (22.77%)	$27,325 (24.64%)	$108,040 (100%)
2017 RETURNS	21.8%	14.7%	25%	9.3%	
TOTALS 12/31/17	$34,104 (25.42%)	$38,616 (28.79%)	$31,563 (23.53%)	$29,866 (22.26%)	$123,857 (100%)
TO RE- BALANCE BACK TO 25% EACH	Sell $566.75	Sell $5,078.75	Buy $1,974.25	Buy $3,671.25	
	$34,104 - $566.75 = $33,537.25	$38,616 - $5,078.75 = $33,537.25	$31,563 + $1,974.25 = $33,537.25	$29,866 + $3,671,25 = $33,537.25	

Source for returns: www.blackrock.com/investing/literature/investor-education/asset-class-returns-one-pager-va-us.pdf; www.reit.com/sites/default/files/returns/DomesticReturns.pdf

Let's assume a starting investment of $100,000, with $25,000 invested in each bucket. The table below shows how each component grows and how that leads to a new percentage allocation by the end of 2016 and 2017. To rebalance back to the 25 percent allocated to four asset classes each, divide the new total assets equally in four and either sell (if one investment has a larger balance than that) or buy (if an investment has less than its equal share) as much as you need in order to reach that level of equilibrium.

Without rebalancing, the portfolio's asset allocation would drift more heavily in the direction of the recent outperforming assets, reflective of their higher rate of return. You could either rebalance smaller amounts after year one or wait for a slightly greater variance and rebalance more substantially after year two.

This exercise forces you to sell assets that have performed well and buy more of those that have performed poorly. That's in contrast with human nature, but instills the discipline to sell high and buy low while staying on track with your asset allocation.

Review and rebalance after major life events. In addition to the regular monitoring and rebalancing exercise that I just described, you should also review your portfolio after major life events, such as marriage, the birth of a child, divorce, or if you begin or leave a job.

For example, if you leave a job, your need for additional cash might increase with less money flowing in. In turn, that might lead you to adopt a somewhat more conservative mix of assets, or you might transfer some money from a longer-term account into a more liquid, short-term investment.

In the case of a marriage, some couples treat their portfolios holistically, looking at their entire asset allocation as a couple. In other cases, each spouse handles things separately, but perhaps with the life change of marriage, associated goals and plans might influence what you save for the future and how.

A rule of thumb you can ignore. To make things easy for some investors, popular financial planning wisdom has some rules of thumb. While some of these "rules" have a certain level of merit, I don't care for a certain one that has become quite popular regarding asset allocation.

It works like this: Subtract your age from 120 (or 110, or 130) to see the percentage of stocks you should own within your portfolio.

At age 40, you'd have 80 percent in stocks (if using 120 as the starting point).

At age 60, you'd have 60 percent in stocks.

At age 80, you'd have 40 percent in stocks.

You see the pattern. Generally, it's recommended to have less and less in stocks and other similarly risky assets as you age and shift to having more and more of your wealth in bonds and cash. While this does have some merit in a broad sense—you shouldn't be too exposed to risk with little time for your portfolio to rebound from a crash—the problem is that everyone is different, and this doesn't factor in your risk tolerance and other critically important questions about your personal situation.

To drive this point home, I'll share a story about a 90-year-old woman named Mrs. Green who I met 20 years ago. At the time, she had $6 million in assets, which would be worth about $20 million in 2018. She had 90 percent of her assets in common stock and was living off the dividends of $120,000 a year. When I told her that I thought she was being too aggressive with this money, she said, "Listen here, sonny. I didn't get $6 million by buying Treasury bills."

Mrs. Green had a point, but more importantly, she revealed to me what the money was for: "You're not investing the money for me. You're investing it for my children and grandchildren."

So, remember, every investor is different and one size doesn't fit all.

COMMON ASSET ALLOCATION MISTAKES TO AVOID

Despite how seemingly simple asset allocation is, people make mistakes involving asset allocation all the time. Here are some common ones to be aware of and try to avoid.

1. Ignoring or not understanding asset allocation. It really is the single most important aspect of investing and should provide a framework for all else.

2. Making ad hoc investment decisions without considering your asset allocation. If you take the time to do a thoughtful asset allocation exercise, keep it in mind as you review and consider investments going forward. Don't think of any investments in isolation, but instead as part of that intentional, strategic mix.

3. Not keeping a portfolio-wide view of your entire asset allocation (not just the asset allocation in any one investment account). Let's say you have four investment accounts: a taxable account, a 401(k), an IRA, and a Roth IRA. Rather than look at the asset mix in each one separately, monitor and analyze your portfolio as a whole.

4. Relying on target date funds without considering what's unique about your situation and investment personality. How does it make sense that every person born in the same year or same five-year block has the exact same allocation to stocks and bonds? One size doesn't fit all. Some will inevitably be more risk tolerant than others. Go a step further and tailor your investments to your risk profile and personality. After all, would you buy an ill-fitting suit off the rack or have it adjusted for a good fit?

5. Not taking advantage of dollar-cost averaging (DCA) while accumulating funds. You can take a lot of volatility out of the most volatile security simply by dollar-cost averaging. When you regularly and periodically buy the same dollar amount of an asset that rises and falls in value, that cushions its volatility. When the price per share is higher, you buy fewer shares at a higher price. When the share price falls, your dollar stretches further, allowing you to buy more shares. Over time, this averages out, lowering the security's volatility and potentially lowering your overall costs.

6. Not scaling down on risk as you approach and then enter retirement. Let's assume that you have a portfolio of 90 percent stocks/10 percent bonds, and you're close to retirement age when the market crashes, with stocks losing one-third of their value. A $2 million portfolio with $1.8 million in stocks is now suddenly worth $600,000 less. You now have $1.4 million, of which $1.2 million are in stocks.

That's a sharp loss that could cause you to radically change your retirement lifestyle or even possibly delay your retirement unless you have a built-in buffer as described above in the discussion on short, medium, and long-term tranches.

7. Cutting back too much on risk. The other extreme can be just as dangerous. If you suddenly cut back to, let's say, 25 percent in stocks and 75 percent in bonds at age 65, you might sharply limit your expected return compared with a more substantial allocation to stocks for the long-term growth portion of your investments. For example, would you want your overall portfolio positioned to earn a safe but low 3 percent or 4 percent a year overall for the next three decades or so? Or, does a potential 6 percent or 8 percent or more per year as a target average annual return sound more enticing, taking into account the tranches and their respective expected returns?

Even in your 60s, 70s, and 80s, you want your long-term investments able to grow at a reasonable rate. Because you only withdraw a fraction of your money each year, the bulk of your retirement savings can keep growing over the longer term despite some shorter-term ups and downs.

8. Not taking fullest advantage of the entire mix of low-correlating assets. What makes diversification most effective is owning a variety of sub-asset classes that have low correlation to one another. In other words, their performance is often not in sync. For example, stocks might rise while the price of government bonds falls. For greatest benefit, think beyond stocks, bonds, and cash.

Within stocks, consider diversifying further into small-cap, mid-cap, and large-cap U.S. stocks; international developed markets; and emerging market stocks. Emerging economies, such as India, China, and Brazil, are often less correlated with the U.S. economy or the economies of the developed markets of the United Kingdom, France, or Germany. The performance of stocks in each of those markets might have less correlation with those in another market, particularly small-cap stocks and those in emerging markets.

Among fixed-income assets, adding some emerging markets bonds and high-yield bonds can complement corporate investment grade and government bonds of a variety of maturities.

Altogether, with so many factors contributing to your overall investment returns, this level of diversification can lower your overall portfolio volatility and lead to better and more consistent long-term results.

SECTION III

How to Transition into Retirement and Beyond

CHAPTER 12

How to Plan for Your Retirement

From the time we enter the workforce, we're encouraged to save for our retirement. If we begin early and save enough, we'll likely be in good financial shape, but what about the details? As you approach retirement, it's time to think about and make a number of important decisions.

Questions to consider include: When should I retire? How should I make the transition into retirement? Should I quit work "cold turkey" or should it be a gradual, phased process? Where do I want to live? What kind of lifestyle do I envision? How do I want to spend my days?

WHEN TO RETIRE

The decisions on when to retire and a lot of other related questions regarding this major life transition are highly personal. There are no universally right or wrong answers. You really need to thoughtfully explore what is right for you.

Here are some factors to consider:

Are you financially ready? Do you have enough saved? Have you done the math? This involves an exercise in retirement budgeting. Draw up a list of monthly or annual expenses and then look at your sources of income. Your retirement savings should be sufficient to fill the gap between your expenses and any other sources of income, such as Social Security benefits and a pension. If not, you may not be financially ready to stop working.

Is retirement mandatory for you? The days of people generally receiving their gold watch at age 65 are long gone, but in certain jobs, such as airline pilots, a mandatory retirement age still exists.

How much do you enjoy your job? Assuming that you have some say as to when you retire, ask yourself how much you enjoy your job. Generally, senior-level management tend to want to work longer, partly because they enjoy their jobs more than lower and middle-level managers, who might feel more stressed and less appreciated.

Is your job physically demanding? Although cognitive decline can be an issue for some people, more often physical limitations or fatigue might lead a physical laborer to retire sooner than, say, an accountant, a lawyer, or a business owner. In an extreme case, professional athletes rarely keep their jobs beyond age 40. They face a very, very long retirement!

Are you yearning for a change? Some people might be happy in their jobs, and physically capable of continuing their work, but they might be lured by another unfulfilled pursuit. Is there something calling you that might indicate that it's time for a change?

What is your family situation like? Sometimes a retired spouse or an ill family member, such as an invalid parent, could lead you to retire sooner than you had planned.

How is your health holding up? Some people plan to work longer, but chronic health issues—such as a heart condition—get in the way.

How healthy are your job prospects? If you lose your job in your late 50s or early 60s, your chances of finding another similar one might be limited. Accordingly, you might find yourself being pushed into early retirement. We'll talk about how to manage a forced or unexpected retirement in the next chapter.

Your homework: If you haven't already run the numbers, do the math to know whether or when you'll be financially ready to retire. Think about what you want. Discuss it with your spouse/partner. Formulate a plan. Make it happen.

The transition to retirement, or life 2.0, can take on any form. Does your personal situation allow for some flexibility, such as phasing into retirement? If so, is that what you'd prefer? What might that look like? Tapering slowly into retirement could work if you own your own business and can gradually delegate more, spend less time working, and perhaps take longer and more frequent vacations. Perhaps you're a professional such as a doctor, dentist, lawyer, accountant—someone with a shared practice. Once you reach a certain age, you might find it very agreeable to work two, three, or four days a week as a transition from five days before you finally retire.

Even large organizations, not traditionally known for their flexibility, have become more accommodative to flexible arrangements of many forms. Does your place of work allow for a move from full-time to part-time work en route to full retirement?

A total career change might be in order as well. I have known some people who have quit a $100,000–$150,000 salary in a high-stress job in favor of a much lower-stress job where they earned half as much for a few years. If you could do that in your early 60s, would you? You could potentially keep earning enough money to get by and not have to tap into your retirement savings account or begin drawing your Social Security benefits for a few years.

Are you aware that for every year you delay receiving your Social Security benefits from age 62 to 70, you'll receive 8 percent more for every month for the rest of your life? We'll address Social Security benefits claiming options in Chapter

14, but there are ample potential long-term benefits awaiting those who delay taking their benefits for just a few years.

Other options include beginning a second career, or another new challenge of some kind. Some people choose to retire completely, and then, after a few years—often motivated by money, boredom, or lack of social interaction—they re-enter the workforce. Any of these decisions are reversible, other than your decision on when to claim Social Security benefits.

Your homework: Think about what you want. Talk to people who have recently retired. Perhaps talk with your human resources department and explore your options.

WHERE TO RETIRE

The world is your oyster, at least in theory anyway. Where would you *like* to retire? Would it be possible to retire there? Are you willing to do the homework and explore a variety of places? Factors to consider in selecting a place to retire include:

Family: Do you have kids and grandkids that you want to be near?

Weather/recreation/culture: Are there certain locations that you're drawn to? Perhaps you have a health condition and must avoid cold weather. Maybe you're lured by the prospect of golfing or sailing 12 months a year.

Cost of living: How important is affordability for your retirement lifestyle? Is paying lower state taxes important?

NOMADS AND SNOWBIRDS

One option for retirees is a nomadic lifestyle—driving around the country in a recreational vehicle either spontaneously or with a regular, planned pattern of destinations. We have clients who have toured the country in an RV for the past 12 years and are now realizing they're ready for a more permanent lifestyle.

We also have clients who sail in the Bahamas all winter and then live in an RV, touring the U.S. during the warmer spring and summer months. We also serve the more typical snowbirds who spend the winters in Arizona, Florida, or Hawaii and live in the Washington, D.C. area the rest of the year. There are so many options and variations. You can try something on for size for a few years and then move on.

Your homework: Do your research. Read up on places that you are thinking of, and vacation in some locations for a couple of weeks or a month in order to "try them on for size." Maybe return there at a different time of year. This could allow you to look critically at what it might be like to live there year-round. If you're thinking of buying an RV, try renting one for a month and see if that lifestyle appeals to you.

LIFE 2.0: A TIME FOR ADVENTURE

The old notion of retirement itself is a bit of an outdated concept, according to many life planners. At age 60, 65, or 70, many of us still have plenty of good years ahead in which we can be learning, growing, earning, discovering, and even re-inventing ourselves.

Do you have an unfulfilled dream? Want to travel the world? Learn an instrument or a new language? Start a new career? Volunteer? Become a consultant, leveraging your expertise or passion? If you didn't need to get up and go to work tomorrow, what would you like to do? How can you make that dream into a reality?

Your homework: Think, explore, read, talk with a life coach, talk with any experts who might be able to add insights; then make a plan and see if you can make it happen, of course while incorporating financial moves to pave the way.

CHAPTER 13

What to Do if Your Retirement is Unexpected

"Life is what happens to you while you're busy making other plans."
—*John Lennon*

The best-laid plans often go awry. You may feel fairly sure that you'll work until a certain age, such as 65 or 70, and retire only when you're good and ready, financially and psychologically. Despite your best intentions, however, "life" can happen to you and force you to exit from the working world earlier than planned.

In fact, roughly half of people (48 percent in 2017) retire earlier than they had planned, according to the Employee Benefits Retirement Institute (EBRI). Almost four in 10 (39 percent) of the retirees surveyed in 2017 retired before they reached age 60. The annual EBRI Retirement Confidence Survey also found that the most common reasons people retire early include:

- Health problems or disability (4 in 10 cited that)

- Work-related reasons, such as a company downsizing or closure, or changes in skills (4 in 10)

- Having to care for a spouse or other family member (14 percent)

The result: Many people retire much earlier than they had thought they would. Compare these two statistics:

- While 38 percent of workers expect to retire at 70 or beyond, only 4 percent of retirees report this to be the case.

- While just 9 percent of workers expect to retire before age 60, 39 percent of retirees actually retired that early.

CREATE YOUR PLAN B

Whether you retire earlier than expected because of health issues, job-related reasons, or you are called into action as a family caregiver, begin to plan now and have a contingency plan. How would you handle a forced retirement? What can you do now to prepare?

Risk management is all about foreseeing potential problems and preparing for them just in case. What can you do today in case of a forced retirement?

ESTABLISH A GOOD-SIZED
EMERGENCY FUND—NOW!

Money is power, but it also can create flexibility and provide you with various options. This is why having an emergency fund is beneficial to living a more financially stress-free life. If you can build a cash reserve that could pay for six to 12 months of living expenses in an emergency, you'll have an easier time handling any curveballs that life throws at you.

This is generally a good rule of thumb in financial planning. Having that cushion of cash could serve as a bridge to get you through a period of not working and not yet being able (or willing) to take your Social Security benefits or begin withdrawing from your retirement account. The longer you wait on both of those, the more financially secure you'll be for the rest of your life.

The size of your emergency fund should be influenced by a number of factors, such as whether your family has one or two income earners. A single income comes with greater risk in the event of a job loss. How much demand is there for your skills and talents? Are you protected by a union?

It can be hard but helpful to look critically at yourself and ask honestly, are you being paid too much given your skills and talents, or is your employer getting a deal on you? Could you earn your current salary elsewhere? If you are at a greater financial risk because of any of these or other factors, keep adding to your emergency fund as a precaution.

SAVE MORE DILIGENTLY FOR RETIREMENT

Even if you clearly plan to retire at age 70 and have everything figured out according to that plan, by accelerating your retirement savings you might be able to take a forced early retirement in stride. Take some time and work with an online calculator and do some "what-if" scenarios to see how much more you could save now for an easier tomorrow. No one ever complains about having saved too much!

For example, let's say you're a 55-year-old empty nester. Your son or daughter just graduated college and your mortgage is paid off. This could be a perfect time to sock away some meaningful money for your retirement while preparing for the unexpected. How much more could you save and what impact would that have? Find out with the help of an online calculator like the one located at the AARP website.

TAKE A TIME-OUT

Assuming that you have a decent-sized emergency fund, and wouldn't panic if you lost your job at age 60, what would you do with the time that money could buy you? The possibilities are almost endless.

You could read and research about things you want to do in your next phase of life. You could speak with a career counselor or a life coach to explore your potential and your interests.

It would be a great time to meet with your financial planner and get some help reviewing and possibly rethinking your financial plans.

It might also be healthy to take a long vacation or even a sabbatical of several months, and let go of your daily concerns for a while so that you can gain the kind of insight and perspective that doesn't happen when you're too busy to smell the roses!

As I have said in previous chapters, if you are laid off at age 60 because of difficulty in keeping up with workplace changes, including technology, it can be a great time to follow your true passion. We've seen 60 year olds who didn't keep up with the latest technology find themselves without a job, yet they were able to reinvent themselves as a college professor. Their years of leadership and management skills made them very valuable in the classroom. Non-financially, it has been great to see a person's self-worth change once they realized the fresh value they could provide in a new realm.

REVISE YOUR FINANCIAL PLAN

If you're looking at a forced retirement a few years earlier than you had expected, work through the numbers and see how you can adapt. Perhaps you could live on less money and create a bridging strategy for a few years to avoid tapping into your Social Security benefits sooner than you'd want. Work with your financial advisor on all aspects of a financial contingency plan.

LOOK FOR NEW OPPORTUNITIES

If forced to retire early, think about how you could make lemonade from this lemon. Here are a few possibilities:

Job hunt. If you have health issues that forced you out of one job, are you able to do another type of job? Could you work part-time? If you left your workplace because of company-specific reasons, could you use your skill set elsewhere? If you prefer to not face the kind of stress you dealt with in your old job, what type of lower-stress and presumably lower-paying job might you be open to?

Volunteer. What types of skills and interests do you have that you could put to use in a volunteer capacity? Think about how you might like to give back to society in a way that would fulfill you.

Pursue your dreams. Here's where you can create your own lemonade recipe. What drives your passion? What unexplored areas exist? Think about things that you've always wanted to do but never found or made the time to pursue. Perhaps writing, photography, a musical instrument, or starting a small business of some kind? Follow your passion whether or not it earns you money. (Although, it'd be even better if you can actually generate income from some new activity that you enjoy!)

ONE IMPORTANT REMINDER:
RESIST TAKING SOCIAL SECURITY BENEFITS EARLY!

Not only will you lock in a smaller benefit than at your full retirement age, but the benefits will also be further reduced if you earn more than $17,000 a year.

For some people, it's simply not an option to delay claiming your Social Security benefits. Yet, if you can delay doing so, and if you expect to live at least until your late 70s or early 80s, you'll be ahead financially in the long run.

Read more about when to take Social Security benefits in the next chapter.

CHAPTER 14

When to Take Social Security Benefits

One of the most important choices you'll make as you prepare to retire is deciding when to begin receiving your Social Security benefits. It's a decision that will permanently and profoundly affect your retirement income for the rest of your life.

If you start to take your Social Security benefits before your full retirement age, the benefits will be permanently reduced by a certain percentage for every month that you take benefits (again, before your full retirement age). Conversely, your Social Security benefits will be increased for every month that you delay when you begin to receive them. Currently, the full benefit age is 66 years and four months for people born in 1956, part of a gradual increase to 67 for those born in 1960 or later.

THE COST OF NOT WAITING

This is the impact of taking benefits early based on a full retirement age of 66.

STARTING YOUR SOCIAL SECURITY RETIREMENT BENEFITS AT:	...WILL RESULT IN A PERMANENT MONTHLY BENEFITS REDUCTION OF:	BASED ON FULL MONTHLY RETIREMENT BENEFITS OF $2,000 PER MONTH AT 66, YOU'D RECEIVE:
62	25%	$1,500
63	20%	$1,600
64	13.3%	$1,734
65	6.7%	$1,866

Below is the advantage of taking benefits on a delayed basis.

STARTING YOUR SOCIAL SECURITY RETIREMENT BENEFITS AT:	...WILL RESULT IN A MONTHLY BENEFITS INCREASE OF:	BASED ON FULL MONTHLY RETIREMENT BENEFITS OF $2,000 PER MONTH AT 66, YOU'D RECEIVE:
67	8%	$2,160
68	16%	$2,320
69	24%	$2,480
70	32%	$2,640

Therefore, if you live until age 90—which 25 percent of women are likely to do—and wait until age 70 to claim benefits, the $640 per month increase in benefits (based on the $2,000 base example in the chart) multiplied by 240 months (20 years) would be worth an additional $153,600. In fairness, you'd have to subtract the value of not receiving the $2,000 a month for the 48 months between ages 66 and 70, or $96,000. However, you'd still be ahead $57,600 by waiting the four years.

The reduction or increase in benefits would also apply to spousal benefits in the event of your death. Considering all of this, the financial advantage or drawback of claiming benefits early or late would continue beyond your lifetime.

PEOPLE IGNORE THIS

Despite these profound lifelong advantages of delaying your Social Security benefits, studies show that the vast majority of people either take their benefits early or at full retirement age. Nearly half of men and 42 percent of women take their benefits as soon as they are able to, at age 62, according to the Center for Retirement Research.

Only a tiny fraction—4 percent of men and 2 percent of women—wait until age 70, even though to do so means they'll be rewarded with a risk-free guaranteed 8 percent per year return for the rest of their life. That's a 32 percent increase in your Social Security benefits for delaying receiving them from age 66 to age 70, according to a study on Social Security claiming trends by the Center for Retirement Research at Boston College.

HALF OF US WILL LIVE 20 YEARS
OR MORE BEYOND AGE 65

The reality is that, based on their life expectancy, most Americans would be financially better off by delaying their Social Security benefits. The latest data published on the Social Security Administration's website shows that the average 65-year-old American male can expect to live to 84.3 and his female counterpart can expect to live to 86.6 years.

Compare that to the so-called "break-even age." That's the age at which if you lived to that point or longer, delaying benefits would have paid off. For every month after that, you'd benefit further and further overall for having delayed retirement benefits from Social Security. According to retirement advice on the Charles Schwab Corporation website:

- The breakeven age for delaying benefits from age 62 to 66 is age 77–78.

- The breakeven age for delaying benefits from 62 to 70 is age 80–81.

- The breakeven age for delaying benefits from 66 to 70 is age 82–83.

Overall, the average person at or near age 65 would live to benefit financially from having delayed their Social Security benefits. This is even more likely for wealthier Americans, who tend to live longer than the average American and much longer than the poorest people, according to various studies. A study by the Boston University School of Public Health found that the wealthiest 1 percent of Americans live an average of 10 to 15 years longer than the poorest 1 percent, who tend to adopt less healthy habits such as smoking and eating a less nutritious diet.

The longevity gap is growing larger still. Another study found that the gap between the life expectancy of the wealthy versus the poor grew by four years during a single generation. In a 2014 analysis in *The Atlantic* titled "Get Rich, Live Longer: The Ultimate Consequence of Income Inequality," author Derek Thompson attributed this to access to better food, more social connectivity, and higher-quality health care.

ONE SIZE DOESN'T FIT ALL

Having said all that, there *are* some exceptions where it actually could make sense to claim your Social Security benefits early. The two main reasons why it might make sense to take benefits early are health-related concerns and financial constraints.

Poor health: If you are in poor health, you might no longer be able to work. You might also not expect to live as long as the average American. If so, you could actually need Social Security benefits to get by if you're no longer earning a salary. In this case, you might be better off claiming Social Security payments now.

Financial constraints: It's possible that anyone could be in a financial bind despite their best efforts. If so, you might need to access any source of income as soon as possible. If this is the case, you'd claim Social Security benefits as soon as you're eligible. However, that scenario doesn't fit with the profile of a typical middle-class millionaire who works diligently to prepare for retirement and who is highly solvent financially through the entrenched good habits of frugal living and diligent saving.

If you don't fit into one of those two groups—ill health or financially desperate—you'll likely benefit from waiting as long as you can to begin receiving your Social Security checks.

There's another reason why you want to be careful about taking your Social Security benefits early. If you're still working or receiving other income, keep in mind that your Social Security benefits will be reduced by $1 for every $2 beyond $17,640 in earnings in 2018. That applies if you're below full retirement age for the full year.

The earnings limit is $46,920 for those who will reach their full retirement age (now 66 years and four months) in 2019. Above that level, Social Security benefits will be reduced by $1 for every $3 earned.

I think that's a very effective incentive to wait at least until after you stop working before you begin to collect Social Security benefits.

CLAIMING STRATEGIES FOR COUPLES

There have been some recent rule changes on how you can claim Social Security benefits. Couples should review their options so that they can maximize their combined benefits. Factors to consider include both of your ages, your health statuses, and respective benefits. A lower-earning spouse could receive a substantial survivor benefit based on a deceased, higher-earning spouse's benefit.

For a couple with similar earnings histories and life expectancy, it might make sense for both spouses to delay their benefits to age 70. But, if there are major differences in work history and earnings, the lower-earning spouse could file earlier while the higher earner waits until age 70. This way, you could get the most out of the higher benefit. In many cases, the husband will have earned more and will predecease the wife, leaving the widow with a substantial survivor benefit, according to resources from the Charles Schwab Corporation.

BENEFITS FOR DIVORCED COUPLES

Many divorced couples may not realize that you can receive benefits based on your ex-spouse's work record if that provides a higher benefit than what you'd receive based on your own work record.

That would have no bearing on what the other ex-spouse would receive for his or her own benefits. It's simply an extension of the spousal benefits entitlement. It's an option if your marriage lasted 10 years or longer, you remain unmarried, you're at least age 62, and you and your ex-spouse are eligible for Social Security retirement or disability benefits.

To learn more about applying for Social Security benefits and about claiming strategies, go to the Social Security Administration's website.

You could consider Social Security benefits as a form of insurance. Why not protect yourself further from longevity risk by delaying your benefits if you are able to, thereby raising your monthly benefits for the rest of your life?

SOCIAL SECURITY'S STATUS

By the way, concerns that some people have about Social Security going broke are largely a misinformed exaggeration. Every year, the Social Security Administration Board of Trustees publishes a report in which they project the solvency of the Social Security trust fund. In the 2017 report, they projected that even without a fix of some kind, the trust fund assets would last until 2034. After that point, there'd still be enough money to pay 77 percent of scheduled benefits.

The solvency of Social Security is fixable. All it would take is Congress to take one or a couple of the following measures:

- Raise the ceiling for Social Security taxable earnings.

- Raise Social Security taxes slightly above their current level of 6.2 percent of earnings.

- Change the cost-of-living adjustment (slightly decreasing future benefits).

- Raise the retirement age above age 67.

- Introduce means testing; payouts to high-income retirees would be eliminated.

It's hard to predict what will happen between now and 2034, but there are numerous ways to shore up Social Security, and even if nothing's done, you'll still receive 77 percent of full benefits beginning in 2034, according to the latest forecasts.

CHAPTER 15
Managing Longevity Risk

The good news is we're living longer.

The bad news: because of that, we're more likely to outlive our money.

Outliving your money, also known as longevity risk, is the greatest fear that retirees have. Yet, it's not something people generally address—or at least, we don't address it very well. Sometimes it gets overshadowed by more visible risks, like market volatility.

A lot of investors get nervous as soon as the stock market enters a volatile period and they lose their bearings, including losing sight of the most relevant risk in long-term retirement investing—outliving your money.

What can you do to stay focused on this much larger issue? Start by sticking with your long-term asset allocation, which should always include some growth assets (stocks, real estate, commodities). Learn to ignore the short-term noise and just ride the market's highs and lows, which shouldn't affect you as long as you don't need to access your money for years. You can take some simple steps to help make it more likely that you'll always have money to pay your bills.

ESTIMATE HOW LONG YOU'LL LIVE

Longevity is a vague concept, but you can get a decent estimate of how long you'll live—and therefore how long you'll likely need your money to last—by taking just a few minutes answering questions on an online "How long will I live?" calculator.

The questions in a typical longevity quiz touch on family health history, your lifestyle, nutrition, exercise, stress level, outlook on life, and habits such as flossing and your use of sunscreen.

Once you have a sense of how long you may live, you'll have a rough idea of how long your money will likely need to last. Let's say you're currently 60 and you expect to live until age 90. If you retired tomorrow, you'd need to fund an estimated 30 years in retirement. The real risk is that you could live longer than that—to age 95, 100, or even longer.

Because of medical advances, the potential for people to live longer and longer grows. Life expectancies could creep up, with more people living well beyond 100 to 110 or 120 or even longer. Talk about longevity risk! I don't want to scare you, but you can see how you need to take this risk seriously.

How can you make sure you won't run out of money even if you live longer than expected?

FIVE WAYS TO MANAGE LONGEVITY RISK

1. Save enough so that you have confidence you can retire and be fine financially. Knowing how much is enough could be a challenge, but the next two steps will help clarify this...

2. Do a retirement budget. The best way to know whether you have saved enough or to know how much you need to save is by doing a fairly thorough *retirement budget*. If you're within a few years of retirement, work with your current expenses as a baseline, making your budget more accurate and enhancing its value as a planning tool.

Tally your current expenses and consider which costs are likely to rise or fall in retirement and by roughly how much. For instance, are you still making mortgage payments? When will you have it paid off in full? Are you paying anything for your children's college or other costs that you don't expect to have in a few years? Some expense areas might not change much, such as food, clothing, utilities, property taxes, and insurance, but some might if you decide to downsize. Furthermore, with no need for daily commutes to an office, you might spend less on transportation. On the other hand, your leisure costs, including travel and vacations, might rise especially in your earlier, more active retirement years. Although, as you age, you'll likely be less active, and these expenses are likely to decline in your 70s and 80s.

Once you've tallied your expenses, list your sources of guaranteed income, including Social Security benefits and any pensions. The gap between your anticipated expenses and your known income sources is what you'll need to fund through your retirement account withdrawals and any other income, such as earnings from a part-time job.

There are many good, handy budgeting calculators available online—I recommend the one on Quicken's website. Creating a retirement budget will help you assess how much you need to withdraw from your retirement accounts each year and whether that will be sustainable based on a "safe" withdrawal rate.

3. *Work within a sustainable withdrawal rate.* Based on research, it's widely accepted that your retirement savings should last 30 or more years if you limit withdrawals to 4 percent or 4.5 percent of your retirement savings in your first year of retirement, and then adjust that for inflation. A handy way to figure out how much you'll need to have saved is to divide the 4 percent or 4.5 percent figure by 100. If you're assuming a safe withdrawal rate of 4 percent, you'd need 25 times the dollar figure of your year-one withdrawals (the gap between your expenses and other sources of retirement income). With a rate of 4.5 percent, it would be 22.2.

If you estimate you'll need $40,000 a year in retirement account withdrawals, if using 4 percent, multiply that by 25 and you'd need to have $1 million saved. For a 4.5 percent withdrawal rate, multiply by 22.2 and you'd need $888,000 saved. If you expect to withdraw $80,000 a year from your savings, you'd need $2 million or $1.776 million saved, based on 4 percent and 4.5 percent, respectively.

It's also worth noting that this "safe withdrawal rate" works optimally with a diversified asset mix of perhaps 50 percent to 75 percent allocated to stocks, generating a decent potential long-term return while managing volatility.[1]

Also to keep in mind, this simple formula is about *not* running out of money, but the assumption that your retirement expenses at age 65 will still hold steady (plus inflation) at age 85 seems a bit conservative. Based on what I've observed, you're likely to spend somewhat less over time. After all, how many 85 year olds do you know are as active as they were at age 65?

In my experience, retirees typically spend their first decade—ages 65–75—traveling and doing fun activities while they're healthy. By their 70s, they tend to grow more focused on their grandchildren's soccer schedule. Once they reach age 85, they are most concerned about when *Judge Judy* or *Oprah* reruns are on TV.

Let's take a more critical look at the 4 percent or 4.5 percent universally touted safe withdrawal rate. It works as a simple rule of thumb, but clearly, not everyone's situation is identical. One of the critical factors is your age when you retire, which determines how long you'll need your money to last.

I often tell people that if you want to retire at age 60, you should consider a withdrawal rate that's closer to 3 percent. For those retiring between 65 and 70, a withdrawal rate of 4 percent makes sense. If retiring in your 70s, your withdrawal rate could be 5 to 6 percent. For those considering a withdrawal rate after age 80, I first ask them how many push-ups they can do and then we determine their withdrawal rate! Seriously, after age 80, your health, the value of your estate, and your desires regarding leaving money in your estate for family and charitable desires will influence a sound withdrawal rate.

4. Annuitize a portion of your life savings. One of the best ways to make sure you don't run out of money is to create a guaranteed stream of income through an annuity. This is one of the most critical and effective ways to make sure you will always have money for your basic costs: Convert enough of your savings into a guaranteed annual income to help supplement Social Security and any other guaranteed regular income such as a pension in paying for your fixed, regular expenses, such as mortgage or rent, insurance, utilities, and taxes.

You can use the retirement savings that are left after you purchase the annuity to pay for variable expenses, including discretionary items.

It's also important to note that not everyone will need to annuitize some of their savings. For example, if you have sizeable Social Security benefits relative to your salary and you receive a pension from your employer, you may have all your essential expenses in retirement covered; or, if you are sitting on a comfortable cushion of wealth, you really don't need to worry about outliving your money.

But for others, it can provide peace of mind to know that no matter what happens to the rest of your investments in a volatile market, your basic expenses will be taken care of for life.

5. Create tranches. In Chapter 11, I discussed the benefits of creating and maintaining segments or tranches of your portfolio devoted to short-term, medium-term, and longer-term tranches. Each of these will have a distinct purpose and investment focus. The short-term segment provides safe access to liquid, stable funds that will see you through a couple of years. The medium-term tranche provides income from bonds and dividend-yielding stocks that will augment your income as necessary for several years to a decade.

Because both of those create an effective buffer against market volatility, you'll be able to invest the rest of your savings with a focus on long-term growth and higher potential returns. You'll be able to ride out any volatility if you're assured of not needing to tap into those investments for a decade or longer. The higher potential returns you can earn, the more your portfolio will grow and potentially last longer.

Monitor your finances annually. All of these elements are things you can and should do before or as you enter retirement—saving, budgeting, not withdrawing too much too soon, annuitizing some money as needed, and creating short-, medium-, and long-term tranches. However, none of these are "set it and forget it." Every year, review your finances and adjust them as necessary.

This should include a review of your life savings, your net worth, your annual and/or monthly budget (update your sources of income and expenses), and your asset allocation as well as the performance of your investments.

Look at each tranche and adjust as needed. For instance, if the balance in your short-term tranche is getting low, transfer some money from the medium-term portion, and similarly from the long-term to the medium-term portions as needed.

In the next chapter, we'll discuss how to manage your retirement income effectively over time and make adjustments as needed.

CHAPTER 16
Managing Retirement Income: Making Adjustments

I n the previous chapter, we discussed longevity risk, or the chance that you could outlive your money. It's a major concern, but it's just one of several things to consider as you manage your retirement income.

Imagine yourself walking a financial tightrope. On the one hand, you don't want to spend your savings too soon and run out of money. On the other hand, you need to make sure you have enough money to live on now. How do you really know you're being frugal enough without cutting back too much? What a shame if you found yourself with plenty of money left in your late 80s or 90s after denying yourself unnecessarily for years.

So, let's see if you can walk that tightrope with the skill and grace of a financial acrobat. It might not be as hard as you think. What could you do to make sure that your money lasts while enjoying it responsibly?

Here are a dozen things you can do to manage your retirement income well:

1. Make sure you're financially ready to retire. You likely won't know you're financially ready to retire until you do a retirement budget and run the numbers. Once you're comfortable with the accuracy of your estimated expenses and calculate a safe, sustainable rate of withdrawal from your retirement account(s), you should have a good idea. Determine your readiness for retirement with Vanguard's retirement calculator: https://investor.vanguard.com/retirement.

If you're in doubt, one option is to consider delaying retirement by a year or two. The combined impact is that you'd have more money available to fund a slightly shorter retirement. In that case, you could potentially enjoy a slightly higher standard of living in retirement. Also consider delaying when you claim your Social Security benefits. You'll boost your lifelong monthly benefit incrementally for every month that you hold off on claiming your benefits.

A second option could be a phased retirement if you're self-employed or a professional, such as a doctor or a lawyer, and can transition gradually by working fewer hours for perhaps a few years. As a third option, consider working part-time for a while after retiring. You can always come back to that if the need or interest arises.

2. Budget, monitor, and revise as needed. If you're within five years of retirement, you can do a fairly accurate retirement budget. As mentioned in the previous chapter, review your current expenses and assess what's likely to change and by how much in retirement. Then, estimate what you'll receive from Social Security and any other income sources. The gap between those two figures is the income you'll need to create from retirement account withdrawals.

However, budgeting shouldn't be a one-and-done activity, even if you expect your retirement expenses and income to be fairly steady. While at least some of your income sources are likely to be stable, any employment income might vary, especially if you're phasing into retirement or working part-time.

More dramatically, your expenses are likely to change from year to year as you incur some one-time costs, such as a big vacation, a new vehicle, or major repairs or renovations to your home. In some cases, paying off your mortgage or paying off an auto loan will lighten your financial load. So, stay on top of changes to your budget by reviewing it at least annually.

3. Hold off as long as you can before withdrawing Social Security benefits. At the risk of repeating myself until I'm blue in the face, this is such an important decision that I am reiterating it one more time. I discussed this in Chapter 14, so I direct you back there for a review of that discussion. There are exceptions, but unless you truly need the money from Social Security at age 62 or at some point before your full retirement age, most people will benefit from waiting because they'll end up receiving more money over the course of their lifetime.

4. Make sustainable retirement account withdrawals. In the previous chapter on longevity risk, I provided a thorough explanation of sustainable or safe retirement account withdrawals. As with budgeting, don't treat this as a one-time "set it and forget it" process. You may have decided on an initial withdrawal rate of 4 percent or 5 percent of your assets. As life in retirement unfolds, you'll need to review all aspects of your situation and evaluate what has changed and how you need to adapt based on your changing expenses and amount of available funds.

5. Account for inflation. One thing that will potentially affect you a great deal in retirement is the rising cost of goods and services, or inflation, which can reduce your purchasing power.

Be proactive by building inflation into your financial plans and projections. Your investment plan should address inflation risk. Include a large enough growth component so that your savings can at least outpace inflation. That means a healthy allocation to stocks. It should also include a variety of inflation-sensitive assets, such as Treasury Inflation-Protected Securities, real estate—either directly or through real estate investment trusts (REITs)—and commodities as part of a broadly diversified mix of investments.

6. Be sure to take your RMDs (even if you don't need them). As if you didn't already have enough to plan and strategize over, once you reach age 70½, you'll need to make sure you withdraw at least your Required Minimum Distributions (RMDs). That's the amount that is mandatory for tax-deferred retirement accounts including 401(k)s and similar workplace retirement savings plans and traditional IRAs. If you fail to take your full RMD from these accounts, you'll have to pay a penalty of 50 percent of the amount that was not withdrawn. It's worth noting that Roth IRAs have no RMD requirements.

Depending on your financial circumstances, you might not actually need your RMDs as retirement income, at least in some years. If that's the case, there are several things you can do. One is to convert some of your traditional IRA to a Roth IRA. This could make sense in a year in which your income has dropped in retirement, but you anticipate your income rising—for instance, in your late 60s if you're pushing off claiming Social Security benefits until age 70. By doing a Roth conversion, you'll lower your RMDs and create more flexibility down the road.

If you're still working while in retirement and also participate in your employer's 401(k), you are not required to take RMDs from that account. However, you do have to take them from your IRAs (including SEP and SIMPLE). Therefore, consider rolling over your IRA account to your 401(k), as long as the tax deferral is more beneficial than the other advantages of having IRAs.

Tax planning is only one aspect of one's financial picture. Estate planning and investment options are equally important considerations. Another option is to buy a qualified longevity annuity contract (QLAC), which is a type of annuity. In addition to providing future guaranteed income, you'll defer RMDs until age 85 on the amount that you annuitize. You could also reinvest the RMD proceeds in a taxable account or a Roth IRA so that you can continue to take advantage of potential growth.

7. Match your fixed costs with guaranteed income. One way to manage your retirement income is to try to match your fixed costs—such as mortgage or rent, monthly car payments, utility bills, auto and home insurance, et cetera—with reliable guaranteed income. Tally your fixed costs and then subtract your Social Security benefits and/or a pension if you receive one. The gap is the amount of income you'd need to create each month to fully take care of your regular, predictable living costs. You could create that monthly income through an annuity that you'd purchase with a portion of your retirement savings.

8. Carefully consider which accounts to withdraw from first. While there's no single, universal best approach, many experts advise holding off as long as possible from withdrawing from your tax-deferred accounts, especially Roth accounts, because your account assets can grow tax-deferred for a longer period.

All the same, everyone's situation is different and one thing you should consider is whether your income is near the upper threshold of your tax bracket. If so, withdrawing from a taxable account might move you into a higher tax bracket. If income fluctuates from one year to the next, do what makes the most sense for any given situation. If you're not sure, talk with your financial advisor.

9. Manage your tranches. If you're segmenting your retirement assets into short-, medium-, and long-term tranches, monitor how much you have in each slice of your portfolio, and adjust as needed. Let's say you want to maintain enough short-term cash to help fund roughly two years of living once you account for other sources of income, such as Social Security.

Let's also assume you need $80,000 to pay for two years' worth of living expenses. Every year or every few months, review your collective account balance in the short-term account(s). Then, transfer money as needed from your medium-term or long-term tranche to maintain that $80,000 threshold.

Similarly, let's assume you want to maintain $300,000 in

the medium tier. If you're transferring $40,000 from there into the short-term tranche, then plan to replace that with a similar amount from your long-term tranche.

10. Be open to a Plan B. In all likelihood, if your finances are healthy and stable, all you'll need to do is tweak things. But, if you need to address more serious financial shortfalls or warning signals, be prepared to act. This could involve cutting back on your discretionary expenses, downsizing, or finding another source of income, such as a part-time job. If you're in a truly serious situation, consider a reverse mortgage.

11. Work with a financial advisor. Just as you would hire a plumber or electrician to help you with home repairs or pay an auto mechanic to work on your vehicle, unless you're highly adept at financial matters, you could probably benefit from working with a professional financial advisor. There's a lot at stake in your financial future, and the challenges and intricacies of making sure you have sufficient income for the rest of your life probably calls on spending a bit of money to make sure you always have enough money to live on.

12. Monitor your financial situation. The theme throughout this chapter on managing retirement income is to stay on top of your finances and make adjustments as necessary. Doing a comprehensive annual financial check-up can provide the structure needed to make sure you address your retirement income needs for today and tomorrow. As part of this annual review, assess your net worth; review the performance of your investments and their asset allocation and rebalance as necessary; review your expenses and income needs; review the sustainability of your assets; and review anything else that deserves some attention now or will in the near future.

CHAPTER 17

Managing Health Care and Long-Term Care Costs in Retirement

In this chapter, we'll discuss one of the biggest concerns facing middle-class millionaires: how to predict and pay for health care. Right behind that is understanding what health insurance doesn't pay for.

With people living longer, even with healthy lifestyles, the total tab for health care costs after you retire could be enormous. Fidelity Investments does an annual survey, and their latest estimate as of 2018 is that the average couple needs to set aside $280,000 in today's dollars for medical expenses in retirement, excluding long-term care.[1] But it's the end-of-life costs—your final five years on this earth—that really jeopardize the ability to provide for your spouse after you pass away. These can easily exceed $200,000 in today's dollars, depending on your needs and whether you suffer from dementia, as they include long-term care services.

Now that I have your attention, let's look at some simple steps to take to protect yourself against the risks of rising health and long-term care costs. First, though, please take a moment if you need to take your high blood pressure pill…

MEDICARE: UNDERSTAND IT, SIGN UP FOR IT

Take the time to learn all about Medicare. It has various parts, and it doesn't cover everything. There are plenty of videos on YouTube that help to explain the various aspects of Medicare. This is a very individualized decision that may change as your life evolves. Factors such as your state of residence and whether you work for a small employer or are self-employed after 65 will come into play. For some personal guidance, including a free consultation, look up the State Health Insurance Assistance Program (SHIP) near you.

Part A: Pays for hospital costs after a deductible and may cover up to 100 days of skilled nursing care during each benefit period after a high daily deductible. While most people don't pay a premium for Medicare Part A, there are high deductibles to meet and complicated rules to understand.

Part B: Optional coverage for medical expenses including doctor visits and medical equipment. The annual premium can vary depending on your income. Also, it only covers 80 percent of "Medicare-approved" costs, assuming your doctor takes Medicare patients. You're responsible for the remaining 20 percent of the cost.

Part D: Optional prescription drug coverage. This also comes with an extra premium.

Medicare Advantage: All-in-one managed care plans. These plans combine Parts A, B, and D and are often offered as a "one-stop shop" by coordinated providers.

Supplemental/"Medigap" policies: There are several versions to consider that help to cover your out-of-pocket expenses or provide coverage while traveling outside of the United States, but none of them cover long-term care expenses, vision, or dental.

It's important to sign up for Medicare B during the seven-month initial enrollment period beginning three months before the month in which you celebrate your 65th birthday. Missing this window could result in a gap in health care coverage and an annual penalty in the form of an additional premium cost. The exception is if you're still working or are covered under your spouse's plan. Be sure it's a large employer's plan because these exceptions don't apply if you're self-employed or work for a small company. Visit the Medicare website or consult with your local SHIP office for help in making a wise decision.

If you retire and sign up for Social Security benefits at age 62, you'll need to come up with a plan to cover your health care costs for the three years before age 65. Options include:

- COBRA
- Accessing your spouse's employer's plan if available

- Signing up for health care on the public marketplace through the Affordable Care Act

- Buying private insurance through a local health insurance agent or a trade or professional association

Be sure to make this decision with your eyes wide open. Often we'll convince our clients to work longer, even if it means taking a less strenuous job for less money, just to retain health insurance benefits until they're 65.

HOW TO GET AHEAD

If your employer offers a high-deductible insurance plan that is "HSA Eligible," you might be able to open a Health Savings Account. HSAs are like an IRA for health expenses. HSA contributions are tax-deductible, the cash can be invested in mutual funds and grow tax-deferred, and the withdrawals are tax-free at any age if used for eligible medical expenses. After age 65, they become tax-free for *any usage*.

So, think of it as an IRA that you can use for health expenses while you're younger and enjoy the benefits of when you're retired as another tax-preferred savings account. Unfortunately, these are still not widely understood and you need to have the excess cash flow to not only save money for the long term, but also be able to pay the high deductible should you need health coverage in the short term.

That brings us to the other very expensive issue facing middle-class millionaires in retirement—long-term care.

HOW WILL YOU PAY FOR LONG-TERM CARE?

Long-term care is becoming more of a concern for our clients and their families. We see it both from the aging parent's perspective and their baby boomer children who are taking care of them while trying to pay for college or weddings for their own children. The perspectives are varied, but they all agree on two things. First, paying someone to take care of a parent is expensive whether at home or in a facility. Second, they want to have the best possible care and lifestyle that suits them.

In order to address these concerns, it's important to educate yourself on the current costs, methods of receiving care, and how you can pay for it, whether it's researching options for your 80-year-old mother or looking ahead for your own needs perhaps 30 years from now.

Many family members naturally want to take care of their parents, but soon realize the toll it takes on them and their own families. They might have to miss work, which would make them less capable of saving for their own golden years, or they might tap into their own savings to pay for caretakers. There's also the emotional toll that comes with caring for a parent, especially if they are mentally ill or depressed.

The key here is to plan ahead and, when possible, hire professional services to help care for your parent so that you can take care of yourself and your own family. This might mean making hard choices like selling a house and moving in with family members, or moving straight to an assisted-living facility that offers independent living and the option to transfer to a skilled care wing later on.

Aging is a gradual process and while many people insist

they'd rather die than need long-term care services, the truth is that many seniors find they can maintain a good quality of life even while they need some day-to-day help. Fortunately, there are many options available and resources to help figure out what you need and when.

Let's start with some basic definitions and cost estimates based on national averages as tabulated by the 2018 Genworth Cost of Care Survey.

Long-Term Care: The type of services provided when one is unable to perform certain "acts of daily living" (ADLs), such as dressing and bathing oneself. It can also be necessary when caring for someone with Alzheimer's disease or advanced dementia.

Home Health Aide: Also commonly referred to as companion caregivers, these are professionals trained to make you feel comfortable and safe in your home. These are often the first helpers we use as we age. They can do everything from running errands to light housekeeping and have a keen eye for potential hazards around the home. They can also keep us company so we can still enjoy daily walks, or help us at the grocery store. They typically charge around $22 an hour and often have a minimum of four hours per visit. They could be self-employed or hired through an agency.

Adult Day Care: These organizations offer a safe place to drop off your loved one for the day while you go to work. They are typically private/public organizations that offer activities and a social setting for seniors. Many even offer transportation services, medical management, and meals.

Visiting Nurse: When you need help administering medications, physical therapy, or wound and injury care, you will need a registered nurse or perhaps certified nursing assistant. These "skilled care" providers charge an average of $28 an hour.[2]

Assisted Living Facility: This type of "community care" provides a continuum of care. They allow seniors to live independently at first in an apartment or small house. But, when residents reach a point where they shouldn't be left alone, they can transition to the nursing home area of the community. These are popular with couples who may have one spouse suffering from mental illness. This allows them to get the help they need while remaining in close proximity. Average monthly costs are $3,750 plus a hefty down payment (often several hundred thousand dollars). They can vary from small, simple facilities with four residents to large hotel-like accommodations for hundreds of people. There may also be waiting lists to get into these facilities, so research this well before you or a loved one actually needs it.

Nursing Home: These traditional facilities care for seniors when they're essentially bed-ridden or need round-the-clock skilled-care and supervision. The national average for a nursing home is about $7,000 per month for a shared room and $8,000 per month for a private room, but costs vary widely based on your location and needs. In metropolitan areas or nicer facilities, the monthly cost can range from $9,000 to $11,000, especially for specialized memory care for those with dementia.

Bottom line: Do your research, have a gut check, and discuss practical options with your family well before you need help getting around in your old age. The goal should be to squeeze out the best that life has to offer while not causing too much emotional or financial stress to your loved ones.

For example, a couple of our clients have been steadily saving their modest teaching salaries and maximizing their employer retirement accounts as well as their Roth IRAs. They're looking forward to retiring soon but had just one more concern weighing on them: They both have relatives with dementia. While they've saved enough to retire comfortably, they know how expensive it is to pay for care, particularly specialized care, and they didn't want their children to go through the emotional stress they experienced with their own parents.

In order to advise them, we educated them about long-term care insurance and introduced them to an insurance broker who specializes in these policies and who could help them navigate the complexities of long-term care insurance. This helped them tremendously to understand their options. Working as a team, we helped them obtain policies they can afford, giving them some peace of mind knowing there's a good chance at least one of them will need some care at some point in their life. Having insurance may not cover all of the future costs, but it will help preserve assets for the surviving spouse and let the children work and save for their own needs, rather than sacrifice for them.

On the flip side, we have a client who by all accounts can self-insure. Her investments have grown, as has her monthly nursing home bill. She is 96 years old and has spent nearly 10 years in a nursing home. Clearly, she's bucking the averages, but at $12,000 per month, her children, who are concerned about soon needing long-term care support themselves, are worried her nest egg may run out and they're in no position to take care of her. However, they're grateful that we invested some of her money for growth, despite her age. Looking back, had they kept all of her assets in cash 10 years ago, she would have run out of money by now.

NATIONAL AVERAGES ON AN ANNUAL BASIS

- Home Health Aide: 44 hours/week, $50,336

- Adult Day Care: five days/week, $18,720

- Assisted Living Facility: $48,000 (not including initial deposit)

- Nursing Home: $100,375 (private room), $89,297 (semi-private)[3]

WILL YOU NEED LONG-TERM CARE?

To put it bluntly, there's roughly a 50/50 chance. Overall, 52 percent of people turning 65 will need some type of long-term care support or services at some point in their lives. On average, they'll need that help for about two years. On the other hand, 22 percent of those individuals will need care for a longer period. This jumps to 31 percent if you're in a lower income bracket. Fourteen percent will need care for up to five years. It's no surprise that most seniors prefer to stay in their home or a home-like setting as long as possible, but the ability to do so depends on their resources or the availability of a friend or family member willing to take care of them. Thus, while the average length of time spent in a nursing home may only be about two years, most seniors will begin needing help gradually or have an accident and then go through a period of rehabilitation at home.

Those who don't have the resources or family support tend to wind up in facilities or have home care paid for by Medicaid or Medicare. In 2013, nationwide we spent $339 billion on long-term care services. Medicaid paid for 43 percent of that and Medicare paid for 22 percent (the initial 100 days discussed earlier).[4]

A couple of final thoughts: The figures cited above are averages. What if you're an unlucky person who incurs higher costs than that? How will you pay for it all?

While a healthy lifestyle can certainly help you live longer, even being healthy isn't a guarantee that your lifetime health care costs will decline. That's because even if you incur fewer health-related costs up front, your good health might lead you to live longer, during which time your health likely will fade at some point, and you could eventually rack up higher health care costs over more years.

So, save, save, save. It just might come in handy!

For further information on this critical topic, there are some great online resources, including the Medicare website—medicare.gov—and various articles on costs at seniorliving.org, genworth.com, and Morningstar.com.

CHAPTER 18
Planned Giving

Personal philanthropy, or charitable giving, is often a life-long pursuit, but it can take on even greater importance in your later years. There are a couple of typical reasons. As we come to terms with our mortality, many of us think about our legacy. Giving meaningfully to the charities of your choice is one way to make a lasting impact. With proper planning, the charitable giving that may have been a major thread throughout your life can continue after you're gone, allowing you to keep making a difference.

By making charitable donations that enable you to reduce your tax burden, more of your money can go to work in the most effective way, supporting your favorite causes even more.

One common characteristic I see among long-term successful middle-class millionaires is that they live their lives in balance, saving at least 10 percent of their earnings, giving 10 percent, and living on 80 percent. When people live below their means—as a saver and a giver—they learn the inner peace of defining success on their own terms. With that in mind, I'm all for gifting to charities with the most bang for the buck, allowing you to make an even larger difference and allowing your money to go even further.

HOW TO MAKE YOUR CHARITABLE
GIVING TAX-EFFICIENT

Navigating the tax rules that govern charitable donations along with gifts to non-charities, such as your family members, and using all the forms of giving to your best advantage is fairly complex. However, with guidance from a financial professional, you can help your charitable dollars do even more good.

There are a few best practices to consider to make the most of annual and lifetime limits on gifting. In addition, by creating the right vehicles, you can help your favorite charities continue to benefit from your generosity after you're gone.

BEST PRACTICES IN LIFETIME GIVING

There are several ways to get the biggest bang for your buck in your lifetime charitable giving. That can mean making charitable donations in which more of your gift goes to work for the charity, or receiving the largest tax deduction or tax benefit for your donation.

Work within the new tax law: The Tax Cuts and Jobs Act passed by Congress late in 2017 effectively changed the landscape for tax-deductible donations by doubling the standard deduction to $12,000 for individuals and $24,000 for married couples who file a joint tax return. That will almost certainly lead to fewer taxpayers itemizing their deductions and not receiving a tax deduction for their charitable giving.

However, there's also an expanded charitable deduction limit of 60 percent of your adjusted gross income (AGI) for charitable contributions made in cash. The existing deduction limit of 30 percent of your AGI applies to all non-cash gifts, such as stocks, real estate, and appreciated goods.

One way to get the maximum benefit in this new tax landscape is to consider itemizing your deductions every other year or every few years. That way, you could contribute more to charities in a year in which you itemize your deductions, and give less in a year that you take the standard deduction. Also note that if you give more than 60 percent of your AGI to charities in one year, you could carry over the excess amount and apply it as an itemized deduction anytime in the next five years.

You can make your charitable donations through regular individual giving or by using a donor-advised fund (DAF), described in greater detail below. One great benefit of the DAF is that you can claim a tax deduction in the year you contribute to the fund, but the money doesn't need to be disbursed to a charity that year.

Give highly appreciated securities: By giving stocks or other securities that have appreciated in value, you can receive an income tax deduction and bypass capital gains taxes on the amount that the security has increased in value. Let's say you gave $5,000 worth of stock on which you had paid $2,000. You'd receive a $5,000 charitable tax deduction and owe nothing on the $3,000 capital gain. That would result in a savings of $450 in federal tax at the 15 percent capital gains tax bracket, plus any state taxes owed on the capital gain.

Maximize your annual gifting allowance: In addition to tax-deductible donations, you can gift up to $15,000 a year to any individual each year without owing gift tax, or up to $30,000 annually per married couple. If you and your spouse wanted to gift $15,000 each to five people in any year, for a total of $150,000, you could do that without owing any gift tax. If you gave more than that, you could draw on your $11.2 million lifetime gift tax exemption ($22.4 million per couple). Note that any amount you use of this exemption will decrease your federal estate tax exemption accordingly as it's a combined exemption.

529 plan gifts: Putting aside money for your grandchildren via 529 college plans can be an effective way to accomplish multiple goals. You can help them pay for college—and encourage them to attend college—while also lowering your taxable estate. One particularly handy feature, if you're looking to gift a large amount of money in any given year, is the ability to pre-gift, or gift up to five years at once. That would allow you to give $75,000 to a single beneficiary in a single year (you and your spouse could give $150,000).

It's a little-known fact that assets in a 529 plan are not included in the accountholder's estate at death. There's also tremendous flexibility as you retain ongoing control of the account and its assets. Therefore, your annual gifts to 529 plans can be viewed as gifts with strings attached because you retain the right to change beneficiaries, and you can reclaim the assets (you would owe a 10 percent penalty along with tax on the account earnings, however). Earnings are otherwise not included in income taxes and assets are not included in your taxable estate.

The bottom line: There are a number of tax-effective ways to give to charities and your loved ones during your life. Be aware of them and use them all as appropriate.

TEACH YOUR CHILDREN WELL: CULTIVATING AND PERPETUATING FAMILY VALUES

A wonderful and highly effective way to create an ongoing charitable legacy is to make philanthropy an established family value and an entrenched family tradition. Start by teaching your children age-appropriate charitable lessons and involving them at various stages of their development. That will help prepare them to carry on your charitable goals and theirs, through various means as part of your estate-planning legacy.

For example, you can introduce young kids to the notion of regularly setting aside some of their allowance for charity. Talk to teenagers about what organizations you support and why. Ask your young adult children for their suggestions on how to allocate the family charitable budget. Involve them in the process of researching potential charities. In addition, by doing some volunteering as a family in the community, you and your children can see first-hand how non-profits use your charitable gifts. Throughout these activities, explain to your children your philosophy of giving—how, why, and how much you give to charity.

DONOR-ADVISED FUNDS OFFER AN
EASY, FLEXIBLE STRUCTURE

Donor-advised funds (DAFs) have many advantages for philanthropically minded families. Compared with private charitable foundations, DAFs are easier and less costly to set up; less expensive to manage; offer a higher tax deduction limit (60 percent of AGI for cash contributions compared with 30 percent of AGI for foundations); and also offer a limit of 30 percent of AGI (versus 20 percent) for tax-deductible gifts of appreciated assets.

There are no obligations to distribute a certain percentage of assets each year. In contrast, private foundations must distribute at least 5 percent of their net asset value annually. On top of that, there are no excise taxes for DAFs, compared with 1 percent to 2 percent a year for private foundations.

In addition, the names of individual donors can be kept confidential in a DAF and grants can be made anonymously, again in contrast with private foundations.

In brief, DAFs are easy to set up, easy to use, flexible, inexpensive, and highly recommended for most charitable families. There's also no need to disperse funds until you're ready to do so, but you can benefit from your tax-deductible contribution to the DAF in the year that you make the contribution.

CHARITABLE TRUSTS

A couple of excellent hybrid or split-interest charitable trusts are very popular and widely used by people who want to support their favorite cause while also leaving a legacy to or benefiting family members. These are charitable remainder trusts (CRTs) and charitable lead trusts (CLTs).

Charitable remainder trusts: In a CRT, you set up the trust and receive an immediate charitable income tax deduction, defer capital gains tax on appreciated assets, and you can reduce your estate tax liability. For a stated period or for your lifetime, the trust can pay out a certain annual amount to you or a family member beneficiary. Once the designated term or payout period is over, the remainder of the trust becomes the property of the charity. If you have highly appreciated property, you can fund it with those assets, and then sell those assets within the trust without paying capital gains taxes.

Charitable lead trusts: The CLT is like a mirror image of the CRT, with the order of the payout recipients reversed. For the term of the trust or your lifetime, if that's the way you structure the CLT, the charity will receive the annual payout, and once the term (or your life) expires, the assets are distributed to your descendants.

Your investment advisor, tax professional, and/or estate-planning advisor can provide guidance on which vehicle might be best suited to you, your personal goals, and your financial situation.

QUALIFIED CHARITABLE DISTRIBUTIONS
FROM IRA ACCOUNTS

As we see individual retirement accounts growing larger and larger, charitable gifting from an individual's IRA makes more and more sense. As mentioned in Chapter 10, on tax diversification, qualified charitable distributions (QCDs) can help you manage your tax liabilities while facilitating your charitable giving.

If you don't need to use your required minimum distribution (RMD)—the money that you're required to withdraw from your IRA each year after age 70½—then you can make a QCD and reduce your taxable income accordingly without having to itemize your tax deductions for the year.

CHAPTER 19

Tax-Efficient Wealth Transfer

E state planning is one of the most critical aspects of financial planning. Yet, it is often neglected because it can involve some difficult decisions and the stigma associated with our mortality. Regardless, it's vital to have a plan in place, keep it up to date, communicate your wishes clearly to your loved ones, and let them know where to find essential documents and phone numbers of your key estate-planning professionals.

THE BASICS OF ESTATE PLANNING

If you're just starting to prepare your estate plan, you need to understand that it involves more than just a will, although that is important. You should also provide guidance for your loved ones in case they need to make decisions for you in the event that you are incapacitated. These include financial and medical powers of attorney and a living will. Make sure all of your estate-planning documents are up to date, particularly concerning your beneficiaries.

Here's an overview of the key elements of your estate plan:

Your will: Even the most basic will must include an executor—someone responsible and trustworthy whose duties will include taking inventory of your assets, selling your property, and paying your taxes. Make sure they're willing to accept this responsibility. If you have minor children, you'll also need to name a guardian who'll be responsible for them until they are adults. This is vitally important so it bears repeating: *Make sure your beneficiaries are always up to date.* Review and possibly revise your will every few years or after any major life event, such as a birth, death in the family, or a divorce.

Living will: If you needed end-of-life medical intervention, would you want to be kept alive at all costs or would you prefer a do-not-resuscitate (DNR) order? Your living will can guide your family and your doctors based on your wishes regarding specifics such as surgery, artificial life support, and pain relief/palliative care. Telling family members verbally isn't enough. You need to put your wishes in writing. When the time comes, your family will be thankful that you did.

Powers of attorney: There are two types of powers of attorney: temporary (helpful if you are traveling and need someone to act on your behalf while you're gone) and permanent. Permanent powers of attorney can cover two main areas: financial and medical decision making.

A medical, or health care, power of attorney gives someone else the authority to make decisions regarding your health care if you are unconscious, mentally incompetent, or otherwise not able to make decisions on your own.

A durable, or financial, power of attorney can give another person or organization the power to act on your behalf in handling financial and business transactions if you are no longer mentally competent because of illness or injury. The key is to put these powers in place *before* you become unable to make your own decisions.

Important numbers to note: In planning for a tax-efficient transfer of your wealth, be aware of the tax exemption limits (currently $11.18 million per individual; $22.36 million per couple) and tax rates, for state as well as federal estate taxes. Roughly one-third of states—18 states plus D.C.—have estate taxes. In addition, each state has its own levels of tax exemptions and tax rates. Try to stay informed as you make your estate planning decisions.

Lifetime gifting strategies: The $11.18 million exemption applies to the combined exemption from lifetime gift tax as well as estate tax. For more details on gifting strategies, see the previous chapter on planned giving.

PUTTING TRUSTS TO BEST USE

Trusts can play a crucial role in estate planning for middle-class millionaires. In the previous chapter, we discussed charitable trusts as an effective way to create a structure that will allow you to fulfill your philanthropic desires and leave money to your family members. There are many other types of trusts as well.

Trusts come in many forms and can be a powerful and flexible tool that you can use in support of a variety of estate planning goals. You can use them to preserve, protect, and transfer your wealth efficiently and privately. Trusts can help you reduce estate tax liability and give you greater flexibility and control over how and when your assets are distributed.

Here's a brief overview of some types of trusts:

- Irrevocable and revocable trusts. A *revocable trust* is one that you can revoke or change. It could be used to keep your assets out of probate and help to provide privacy and allow for your estate to be settled efficiently. There are also many types of *irrevocable trusts*, in which you no longer control the assets in the trust and the trust can't be amended, modified, or revoked. The benefits of an irrevocable trust typically include reducing your estate taxes and protecting your assets from creditors.

- The most common revocable trust is a revocable living trust, which allows you to remain in control of your assets while empowering another person to serve as your co-trustee or successor trustee in case you need help managing your assets if you should suffer an illness or become less competent. Living trusts are funded by you during your lifetime. They can be used to own a life insurance policy, sheltering it from taxation, in the case of an *irrevocable life insurance trust (ILIT)*. On the other hand, they could allow you to receive gifts in a tax-favorable manner. For example, a *qualified personal residence trust (QPRT)* may allow you to transfer your home or vacation home out of your estate while also allowing you to use the property for a specified period. A *grantor retained annuity trust (GRAT)* would transfer your assets to a trust; in return, you would receive a fixed annuity payment for a period of years.

- Navigate a second marriage with a QTIP. Deciding how to handle inheritance in the case of a second marriage can be tricky. One common solution is a *qualified terminable interest property (QTIP) trust*. It can pay the surviving spouse an annual income during his or her lifetime, after which the remaining assets would be distributed to surviving children, often from a previous marriage.

- *Testamentary trusts* are irrevocable as they aren't created and funded until after the trust's creator dies.

There are numerous other types of trusts with very specific purposes and benefits. Clearly, this is a specialized and complex area and it pays to work with an experienced estate-planning professional to avoid mistakes and achieve the greatest benefits.

A NOTE ABOUT THE USE OF LIFE INSURANCE AS AN ESTATE-PLANNING TOOL

As mentioned above, a life insurance policy placed in a trust—an irrevocable life insurance trust (ILIT)—can be an effective component of an estate plan. It can reduce the size of your taxable estate while adding liquidity, versatility, and income replacement for your family when you die. Remember that the insurance policy *must* be owned by the trust rather than the insured. Otherwise, the assets would be included in your estate, subjecting them to estate taxation.

Managing income tax as well as estate tax liability: It's important to view your full tax liability and work effectively to lower the total amount your estate might owe.

For example, many middle-class millionaires are creating their wealth through retirement accounts. Special care must be taken to name the correct beneficiary or beneficiaries on each retirement account to allow the tax-deferred nature of these accounts to continue. Heirs of your retirement accounts are determined by beneficiary forms, not your will or a trust document. The exception is when a retirement account names a trust as a beneficiary of the account. Whether it's an IRA or employer's retirement plan, the beneficiaries should be reviewed every couple of years.

Make sure you talk with an advisor—not naming the correct beneficiary of a retirement account can be a very expensive and painful mistake. If you're fortunate enough to have an estate worth more than $11 million with most of the money in a retirement account, that account could be subject to 40 percent estate taxes in addition to 35 percent to 39.6 percent income tax rates on a traditional IRA or 401(k) account. In a worst-case scenario, the ultimate beneficiaries of a very large retirement account (that went through probate) would only receive 20 to 25 cents on the dollar in retirement account assets. Proper estate tax planning could save your heirs millions of dollars.

There are a variety of ways to lower your income tax and

estate tax liabilities for an individual with more than $11 million, or a couple with more than $22 million in their taxable estate. One lifelong strategy is to aggressively gift the allowable $15,000 per person ($30,000 per couple) per year to each designated beneficiary. People with large retirement accounts should consider converting traditional retirement accounts to Roth accounts. The income tax liability will substantially reduce the net assets within the taxable estate. Instead of seeing all that money go to taxes, the beneficiaries would inherit the best asset: the Roth account, which can continue to grow and appreciate tax-free and with tax-free distributions.

COMMUNICATION IS KEY

Finally, and I can't stress this enough: Communicate your intensions clearly and well ahead of time. Keep your family well-informed of your plans, intentions, reasoning, where important papers can be found, and who to call for help when the time comes. Make every effort to keep your passing as painless as possible for your loved ones.

SOME FINAL THOUGHTS ABOUT THE
MIDDLE-CLASS MILLIONAIRE

The middle-class millionaire sees personal finance as a lifelong process. The fact that they have $1 million or more in net worth or in investable assets—or in some cases $5 million or $10 million—is just a detail. Money does not define the middle-class millionaire. Money is simply a tool that they can use to enhance their lives.

Middle-class millionaires may differ in a variety of ways, but what they all have in common is they know that success is not a destination. Success is the middle-class millionaire's journey.

I hope that this book teaches you some valuable lessons that you can apply to your personal finances no matter where you are on your journey, and I hope it inspires you toward success.

GLOSSARY

Active Management/Passive Management: Investment assets are either actively or passively managed. In active management, the portfolio management team attempts to perform better than its benchmark index by actively buying and selling securities. Passive management attempts to replicate the returns of a benchmark.

Annuities/Annuitize: An *annuity* is a financial product in which the annuitant (person buying the annuity) purchases a stream of guaranteed income, typically for life. One way to provide some form of guaranteed income for life is to *annuitize* some assets so as to make sure you'll have a stream of income, in addition to Social Security benefits, throughout your life. Annuities can be fixed or variable; deferred or immediate.

Asset allocation: The act of creating a mix of portfolio assets that reflects your individual timeline, risk tolerance, and goals for retirement, among other factors.

Bond coupons: The amount of income you will receive from a bond.

Bond duration: The degree of sensitivity of a bond to interest rate movement. A bond's duration closely reflects its maturity. The longer its duration, the more a bond will be affected by interest rate movement.

Capital gains and losses: When a security appreciates in value or loses value, it incurs a capital gain or loss. However, that gain or loss isn't realized until the security is sold. During the tax year, if you realize a capital gain and expect to owe capital gains tax, one way to reduce your tax liability is to sell another investment for a capital loss, thus offsetting the gain.

Certificates of deposit: Certificates of deposit are the most conservative form of investing. They are typically issued by banks and are guaranteed, but also typically pay low rates of interest.

Charitable trusts (CRTs, CLTRs): Charitable remainder trusts (CRT) and charitable lead trusts (CLT) provide a stream of income during one's life after which the remaining assets are passed on to a beneficiary. In a CRT, a charity receives the end-of-life proceeds. In a CLT, a charity receives a stream of income during one's life.

COBRA (Consolidated Omnibus Budget Reconciliation Act): COBRA gives employees the right to retain group health insurance should they lose their job. However, former employees must pay their own premiums.

***College savings accounts–529 college plans, custodial
accounts:*** College savings accounts can take a number of
forms. The two most popular are 529 state college savings plans
and custodial accounts: Uniform Gifts to Minors Act (UGMA)
and Uniform Gifts to Minors Act (UTMA).

Commodity: A raw material or agricultural product that can be
bought and sold. Commodities are a form of alternative asset
that can help to diversify an investment portfolio because of
their low correlation with other assets.

Correlation of assets: The degree to which two or more assets
tend to perform similarly. High correlation means their prices
behave very similarly. Low or negative correlation can enhance
risk management through greater diversification.

Credit ratings: A credit rating is an evaluation of the credit risk
of a prospective debtor. The issuers of bonds, such as companies
and governments, are rated according to their assessed level of
riskiness based on their credit rating.

Dividends: The regular payment of a designated share of profits
by a company to its shareholders on a per-share basis.

Dollar-cost averaging: The practice of investing the same
dollar amount at regular time intervals, such as once a month.
By buying the same dollar value, you purchase more shares
when the price falls and fewer shares when it rises.

Donor-advised funds: A form of charitable giving in which donors can make a tax-deductible donation and have it invested in the donor-advised fund until a charitable distribution is made, possibly in a later year.

Fiduciary: A person who acts on behalf of another person or persons to manage assets. A fiduciary has a legal and ethical responsibility to act in good faith and trust.

Health Savings Accounts (HSAs): A savings account dedicated to paying for medical costs. HSAs are tax-deductible, and earnings are tax-free. In addition, withdrawals for qualified expenses are tax-free.

Insurance: This includes life insurance, liability insurance, and umbrella insurance. Life insurance is typically sold as a term (finite period) policy or permanent insurance (whole life/universal life). Liability insurance protects against risks of liabilities imposed by lawsuits and similar claims. Umbrella insurance is a form of liability insurance that goes beyond what is covered by other policies, such as auto and homeowners insurance.

Leverage: The use of borrowing money when investing. Leverage can magnify your potential investment losses as well as your potential gains.

Lifetime gifting: The act of giving assets to family members throughout your life rather than passing them on upon death.

Living trust: A trust that is created during your lifetime. It spells out your wishes regarding your assets, dependents, and your heirs.

Living will: A written statement detailing your desires regarding your medical treatment in the event that you are no longer able to express your informed consent, also known as an advance directive.

Longevity risk: The risk of outliving your money.

Medicare: A single-payer national health insurance program that covers seniors and is composed of various parts including hospital insurance, medical insurance, as well as prescription drug coverage.

Money market funds: Mutual funds invested in short-term debt securities, such as U.S. Treasury bills and commercial paper. Money market funds are conservative, short-term investments.

Power of attorney: Written authorization for someone to act on behalf of another person in financial, medical, or other legal matters.

Price-to-earnings ratio, price-to-book ratio, price-to-sales ratio: Forms of stock valuations that use multiples or ratios that divide the stock's estimated value by a metric such as earnings, book value, or annual sales.

Private mortgage insurance: A form of additional monthly insurance that typically is charged to home buyers who don't have a minimum 20 percent down payment on their mortgage.

Qualified charitable distributions: An otherwise taxable distribution from an IRA (other than an ongoing SEP or SIMPLE IRA) owned by an individual who is age 70½ or older that is paid directly from the IRA to a qualified charity.

Required Minimum Distributions (RMDs): Mandatory withdrawals from an IRA, SIMPLE IRA, SEP IRA, or retirement plan account when you reach age 70½.

Revocable/irrevocable trusts: A revocable trust has provisions that can be altered or canceled by the trust's grantor (the person who creates the trust). An irrevocable trust can't be modified, amended, or terminated without the permission of the trust's beneficiary or beneficiaries.

Securities: Investments traded on a secondary market. The most well-known examples of securities are stocks and bonds.

Stock valuation: Methods of calculating theoretical values of companies and their stocks.

Target-date funds: Mutual funds or collective trust funds designed to provide a simple investment solution through a portfolio whose asset allocation mix becomes more conservative as the target date (typically one's projected retirement date) approaches.

Tax-deferred accounts: Accounts (typically retirement accounts) in which investment earnings—including interest, dividends, and capital gains—accumulate tax-free until the investor takes distributions.

Tax loss harvesting: The process of selling an investment that has experienced a loss. By realizing, or "harvesting," a loss, investors are able to offset taxes on capital gains and/or general income.

Testamentary trusts: A trust contained in a last will and testament that provides for the distribution of all or part of an estate.

Tranche: Usually used when referring to money, a *tranche* is a section or portion of something.

ACKNOWLEDGMENTS

I've wanted to write *Middle-Class Millionaire: Surprisingly Simple Strategies to Grow and Enjoy Your Wealth* for a long time. I am grateful and excited this vision has come to life and want to thank everyone who has helped me get here.

Thank you to Allan Kunigis. This book would not be possible without your collaboration, research, and writing expertise.

Thank you to my wife, Diane, and my children, Whitney, Kelly, Ryan, and Megan, for your input and enthusiasm for the book.

And last but not least, thank you to my late father, Cliff Kendall, who inspired and encouraged my passion by helping me buy my first stock with the proceeds from my grass-cutting business at the young age of 12; and of course, my mother, Camille Kendall, who taught me the passion for helping others. Thank you for your love, endless support, and encouragement.

NOTES

CHAPTER 1

1 Matthew Michaels, "18 Celebrities Who Were Rich and Famous before Losing All Their Money," *Business Insider*, May 14, 2018, https://www.businessinsider.com/rich-famous-celebrities-who-lost-all-their-money-2018-5.

2 Dan Caplinger, "If I Make $60,000, How Much Will Social Security Pay Me?" *The Motley Fool*, July 16, 2017, https://www.fool.com/retirement/2017/07/16/if-i-make-60000-how-much-will-social-security-pay.aspx.

3 "401(k) Calculator," Dinkytown.net, KJE Computer Solutions, Inc., n.d., https://www.dinkytown.net/java/401k-calculator.html.

CHAPTER 2

1 Alexandra Twin, "For Dow, Another 12-Year Low," *CNN Money*, March 9, 2009, http://money.cnn.com/2009/03/09/markets/markets_newyork.

2 Twin.

3 "Stock Indexes: Closing Data Bank," Market Data Center, December 29, 2017, *Wall Street Journal*, http://www.wsj.com/mdc/public/page/2_3022-usclosingstk-20171229.html?mod=mdc_pastcalendar.

CHAPTER 3

1   President's Advisory Council on Financial Literacy, 2008 *Annual Report to the President Executive Summary*, January 2009, https://www.treasury.gov/about/organizational-structure/offices/Domestic-Finance/Documents/exec_sum.pdf.

2   Alan Greenspan, "The Challenge of Central Banking in a Democratic Society" (speech, the Annual Dinner and Francis Boyer Lecture of the American Enterprise Institute for Public Policy Research, Washington, DC, December 5, 1996), https://www.federalreserve.gov/boarddocs/speeches/1996/19961205.htm.

3   James K. Glassman, "3 Lessons for Investors from the Tech Bubble," *NASDAQ.com*, February 11, 2015, http://www.nasdaq.com/article/3-lessons-for-investors-from-thetech-bubble-cm443106.

4   Matt Phillips, "Here's How Warren Buffett Made $3.1 Billion on His Crisis-Era Bet on Goldman Sachs," *Quartz*, March 26, 2013, https://qz.com/67052/heres-how-warren-buffett-made-3-1-billion-on-his-crisis-era-bet-on-goldman-sachs.

5   Tanza Loudenback, "24 Mind-Blowing Facts about Warren Buffett and His $87 Billion Fortune," *Business Insider*, August 30, 2018, https://www.businessinsider.com/facts-about-warren-buffett-2016-12.

CHAPTER 4

1   Programme for International Student Assessment, R*esults from PISA 2015 Financial Literacy: United States*, Organisation for Economic Co-operation and Development, n.d., https://www.oecd.org/pisa/PISA-2105-Financial-Literacy-USA.pdf.

CHAPTER 6

1   "Compare Side-by-Side: 2019 Porsche 911 Turbo and 2019 Audi A3," Energy Efficiency & Renewable Energy, US Department of Energy, accessed March 6, 2019, https://www.fueleconomy.gov/feg/Find.do?action=sbs&id=40366&id=41154.

CHAPTER 7

1   "Plan for a Long Retirement," Saving for Retirement, Vanguard, accessed March 6, 2019, https://personal.vanguard.com/us/insights/retirement/plan-for-along-retirement-tool?lang=en.

CHAPTER 8

1   CollegeBoard, *Trends in Higher Education Series: Trends in College Pricing 2017*, October 2017, https://trends.collegeboard.org/sites/default/files/2017-trends-in-college-pricing_1.pdf.

2   All calculations here were done with this online college savings calculator: "College Savings Calculator," Dinkytown.net, KJE Computer Solutions, Inc., accessed March 6, 2019, http://www.dinkytown.net/java/CollegeSavings.html.

CHAPTER 10

1   "5 Primary Tax Benefits to Donors," American Endowment Foundation, accessed March 6, 2019, https://www.aefonline.org/tax-benefits.

CHAPTER 15

1   Wade Pfau, "The Trinity Study and Portfolio Success Rates (Updated to 2018)," Forbes, January 16, 2018, https://www.forbes.com/sites/wadepfau/2018/01/16/the-trinity-study-and-portfolio-success-rates-updated-to-2018/#5634e34c6860.

CHAPTER 17

1   "How to Plan for Rising Health Care Costs," Fidelity Viewpoints, Fidelity, April 18, 2018, https://www.fidelity.com/viewpoints/personal-finance/plan-for-rising-health-care-costs.

2   "The Cost of Senior Care," editorial, Care.com, May 4, 2018, https://www.care.com/c/stories/10237/cost-of-senior-care.

3   Based on Genworth's 2018 Cost of Care Survey: Carescout, Cost of Care Survey 2018, Genworth, June 2018, https://www.genworth.com/aging-and-you/finances/cost-of-care.html.

4   Vivian Nguyen, *Fact Sheet: Long-Term Support and Services*, AARP, March 2017, https://www.aarp.org/content/dam/aarp/ppi/2017-01/Fact%20Sheet%20Long-Term%20Support%20and%20Services.pdf.

$\mathscr{M}$IDDLE-CLASS MILLIONAIRE

SURPRISINGLY SIMPLE STRATEGIES TO GROW AND ENJOY YOUR WEALTH

CLARK A. KENDALL

CFA, AEP®, CFP®

FOUNDER AND CEO OF KENDALL CAPITAL

www.mascotbooks.com

Middle-Class Millionaire: Surprisingly Simple
Strategies to Grow and Enjoy Your Wealth

For more information, please contact:
Mascot Books
620 Herndon Parkway, Suite 320
Herndon, VA 20170
info@mascotbooks.com

Library of Congress Control Number: 2019901806

CPSIA Code: PREFRE0419A
ISBN: 978-1-64307-451-1

Printed in Canada